The Relentless Startup

Published by Spines
ISBN: 979-8-89569-936-2

The Relentless Startup

A Handbook for Hardcore Entrepreneurs

First Edition

Charles Fisher

WARNING

This book is for ambitious entrepreneurs only. The ideas inside are dangerous and could harm your career if you try to apply them within a large, legacy organization.

Contents

How to Use This Book · ix
The Relentless Founder's Manifesto · xv
Preface · xvii

Part One
Preparing Yourself

1. What do you want to achieve? · 3
2. What are you uniquely good at? · 10
3. What's your natural working style? · 22
4. What do you value? · 34
5. Who do you like working with? · 45
6. Are you able to lead? · 56

Part Two
Hiring Others

7. Typical roles in a startup. · 63
8. Let the right ones in. · 68
9. Move the wrong ones out. · 88
10. Leave the chair empty. · 100
11. Beware those with manageritis. · 105
12. Only wimps whine about psychological safety. · 115
13. Grade A treatment for A-players. · 123
14. What do you care what investors think? · 128
15. Chairman of the bored. · 152

Part Three
Building

16. Principles are more important than plans. · 161
17. Prioritize ruthlessly · 169
18. You must decide! · 180
19. The rule of four · 187
20. That word doesn't mean what you think it means · 196

21. Manage to your advantage   204
22. Keep meetings to a minimum   214
23. The first version always sucks   220

Part Four
Protocols

24. Practical steps   231
25. Examples   238
26. Further reading   261
    Conclusion   263

How to Use This Book

I want to be crystal clear about who this book is for, and who it isn't.

This book is for founders who want to build ambitious, world-changing companies and don't give a shit about conventional wisdom. If you're ready to run through walls to achieve your vision, if you understand that most business books are filled with useless platitudes that don't apply to startups, if you want to learn how to be an unstoppable force of nature—then this book is for you.

This book is not for soft people. If you're looking for advice about work-life balance, creating a fun workplace culture, or making everyone feel comfortable, put this book down immediately. There are plenty of other business books filled with that startup killing bullshit. This is a guide for building companies that move with extreme urgency and intensity. Companies that actually get things done. It's for people who measure themselves by their impact, not their popularity.

Part 1 is about you. Read it before you even think about starting a company. Be brutally honest with yourself as you go through the exercises. Starting a company is volunteering for a decade of pain—you better make damn sure you're built for it. If you've already started your company, read this section anyway. You need to understand yourself before you can build a company around your strengths.

Part 2 is about hiring. Your company will only be as good as the people you bring in. Read this section before making your first hire. Then read it again before every major hiring decision. Getting the wrong people on your team is like injecting poison into your company's bloodstream, and most people are the wrong people. The antidotes in this section will help you avoid that fate.

Part 3 is your tactical guide for building. Keep it close. Reference it often. When you're stuck on a decision, when your board is pressuring you to do something stupid, when your team is moving too slowly—come back to these principles. They'll help you stay on track.

Part 4 contains the specific protocols and examples you'll need. Don't read it cover to cover. Use it as a reference manual when you need to implement something from Parts 1-3.

Nearly every piece of management advice you've ever heard will ruin your life if you're running a startup. Building a startup requires you to ignore almost everything taught in business school. Most business books are written by consultants or academics who've never built anything. Or worse, they're written by executives from big companies who never knew, or have long since forgotten, what it takes to move fast and break things.

This book is different. It's written by someone who's been in the trenches, who's made the mistakes, who's learned the hard way what works and what doesn't. The advice here won't make you popular with the majority of people. But it will help you build something great.

If you're ready to be relentless and to fight to change the world, turn the page. If you're looking for a cushy existence where you can make money and don't care about ever moving the needle on anything important, there's always McKinsey.

To my father. He waged a 13 year long war against cancer. He showed me what it truly means to be relentless. This book is for everyone fighting important battles.

The Relentless Founder's Manifesto

We believe that great companies are built around their founders, not in spite of them.

We build our organizations to amplify our strengths, not to hide our flaws.

We do not apologize for who we are.

We envision dramatic changes that will topple the status quo, not fitting in just to get rich.

We stay deep in the details where we excel, rather than retreating to upper management.

We do not apologize for what we know.

We hire for agency, decisiveness, and attitude, not for prior experience or credentials.

We craft policies to reward our strongest teammates, not to prop up the weakest.

We do not apologize for who we like.

We focus intensely on the single most important thing right now, not a list with many priorities.

We keep teams small so they can decide and act quickly, rather than waiting to reach consensus.

We do not apologize for moving fast.

We enforce radical transparency and always tell the truth, not what makes people comfortable.

We are relentless about building unimaginably amazing products, not fulfilling feature requests.

We do not apologize for changing the world.

Preface

I had no idea what I was doing when I started my first company, Unlearn.AI. I knew a lot about science and technology, of course, having studied biophysics in college, in graduate school, and in multiple postdoctoral research positions. I also knew something about our target customers, having spent a year in the pharmaceutical research industry at Pfizer. And I had a small taste of startup life while working at a virtual reality company for a few months in San Francisco. But I knew next-to-nothing about what it would take to start and build a technology company. For me and my co-founders, it was our first rodeo.

Through some miracle, and a lot of hard work, we managed to build something real despite knowing next-to-nothing about how to do it properly. We invented new technologies. Launched entirely new product categories. Navigated government bureaucracies to get regulatory qualifications. Landed multi-million dollar contracts. And raised well over $100M in venture capital. Then, after nearly 8 years running my company as founder and CEO, I fired myself.

Stepping down as CEO from the company I founded while still having the support of our board of directors and investors was an unusual, and not entirely popular, decision. It was a complicated decision and I'm not going to go into the details here. Suffice to say, at the time I thought it was the best thing for both the company and for myself. Like all first time founders, I made many mistakes along the way. But this book is not a memoir or an autobiography, and I don't intend to use these pages to relitigate either my past missteps or triumphs. Instead, this is the book I wish I'd had when I first started out as an entrepreneur. A book by a first time entrepreneur, for first time entrepreneurs. An unapologetic handbook for relentless, mission driven founders containing 8 years of scar tissue worth of accumulated wisdom.

I hope you will use it to build something great.

Startups are different from other types of businesses. It's not just because they tend to start off small. There are lots of small businesses that aren't startups, and there are some startups that haven't yet graduated to the realm of "real businesses" even though they employ thousands of people. Startups are different from other types of businesses because they involve an enormous amount of uncertainty paired with huge ambitions. Uncertainty and ambition are the defining characteristics of a startup.

Preface

As a scientist, I like to think of a startup as a kind of experiment in building a business. It might work, or it might not. And by work, I mean become a gigantic world-changing company. It's not worth taking on so much uncertainty if you're only aiming for small outcomes. If a startup is an experiment, then the only way to know if it will work is to run that experiment and try to build the company.

Each startup begins as a set of hypotheses. For example, Elon Musk may have had the following three hypotheses in mind in the early days at Tesla:

1. It will be possible to design and engineer electric cars that are fast and cool looking.
2. People will want to buy these electric cars because they are fast and cool looking.
3. It will be possible to manufacture these fast and cool looking electric cars at a low enough cost, and in sufficient quantity, to create a profitable business.

If any of these hypotheses was wrong, then Tesla would not have been successful as an electric car company. But these were just some of the big, fundamental hypotheses underlying the basic concept for the business. There were certainly hundreds, thousands even, of smaller hypotheses about how to accomplish these things, because they'd never been done before.

A startup may have technology risk, meaning that it's uncertain if the necessary technology can even be built. It may have market risk, meaning that it's pretty clear the technology can be built but it's not clear that anybody will want the resulting product. Biotech startups working to discover new drugs are often good examples of companies with lots of technology risk, but little market risk. On the other hand, many startups that create software applications are good examples of companies with lots of market risk, but little technology risk. Startups that are doing something really new and ambitious, like Tesla (and, in my opinion, Unlearn.AI), have both.

The job of a founder is to test each of these hypotheses about your business as quickly as possible. The pathway to achieving your vision isn't known, you have to find it. The only way to find it is to experiment. And the more experiments you can run, the more likely you are to find your way. Speed is the superpower of the startup.

How is it possible that a startup ever outcompetes a larger, established company? In some cases, the larger company simply lacks the vision to go after the same problem; perhaps due to an innovator's dilemma. For the sake of argument, however, let's assume that's not true. In general, larger companies have more capital, more people, more brand recognition, more influence, more resources—more of everything! But large companies cannot move quickly, because they cannot make decisions quickly. And after they've made a decision, it takes a lot of time and effort to align their many employees to start moving in that direction. Large ships have a large turning radius. That's the only thing a startup can do better than a large company—make quick decisions and get moving! The ability for a startup to compete is proportional to how quickly it can make decisions and change directions, because that's the limiting step that determines the rate at which you can experiment.

You need to optimize your company for making decisions quickly, for acting quickly, for testing ideas quickly. Speed, speed, speed! This imperative leads to a fundamental law of startups that every founder eventually discovers for themselves —you can get much more done with a few hardcore employees than with many average ones.

Serial entrepreneur Justin Kan has said "First time founders are obsessed with product. Second time founders are obsessed with distribution." [1] I disagree. In my opinion, it's true that first time founders tend to focus on [technology, product, marketing, business model, etc], but second time founders should focus on people.

By focusing on people I don't mean that founders should try to mold themselves into HR professionals, I don't even mean that they should spend much of their time working to build their leadership or management skills, and I definitely don't mean that they should try to create a company where everybody would love to work. Instead, I mean that founders should spend much of their time making sure they have the "right people" on their team.

What does it mean for someone to be one of the "right people" for your startup? That is the billion dollar question. If you answer it correctly, your startup has a massive head start. Of course, the specific attributes of the "right people" will vary depending on your business. But there are three non-nego-

---

1. https://x.com/justinkan/status/1059989657218248704?lang=en

qualities. First, the "right people" fit well with your natural leadership and working style. Second, the "right people" are aligned with your mission and vision for the company. Third, the "right people" have strengths that complement your strengths.

You may have noticed that I've defined the "right people" relative to you. You are the founder of the company after all. And, life's too short to work with people you don't like working with.

The idea that you need to adjust your leadership and working style to accommodate many different types of people—people with different personalities and values—comes from large companies where you can't choose your colleagues. But you can't accommodate everybody without losing a piece of yourself in the process. And if you chip away at yourself enough, you'll eventually find that there's nothing left. If that happens, you will burn out. Guaranteed. But you're an entrepreneur. So you get to choose the people you work with. And there's nothing more important for the future of your startup than getting it right.

I've come to believe that almost all of the advice I received while building my startup was wrong. Almost every book I read about management was bullshit (and I read a lot of them). These books are filled with ideas from leaders at large, legacy companies that will be actively harmful to you and your startup if you try to apply them to your world of high ambition and uncertainty. Startups are different from both large companies, and small businesses.

I'm not alone among founders in thinking that most of the advice I got about how to build my company was terrible. For example, Emery Wells, the founder of Frame.io, laid out five pieces of advice he received that were "glaring misdirections" [2] :

1. Focus only on executive tasks, not product involvement. But, neglecting the core product can undermine the company's value.
2. Decentralize decision-making to scale. But, decentralization can lead to slower action in complex organizations, where centralized leadership is more effective.
3. CEOs shouldn't get caught up in details. But, staying detached from the details ignores the successful hands-on approaches of top leaders.
4. 10X engineers are a myth. But, dismissing high performers can harm productivity, as key individuals often drive the majority of outcomes.
5. Always validate decisions with customer research. But, over-reliance on research can stifle innovation; intuition and personal vision are equally valuable.

When I saw his post for the first time, my jaw hit the floor. I wasn't alone! These were some of the same pieces of stupid

---

2. https://x.com/emerywells/status/1783335501015203986

advice that I'd been getting and, unfortunately, listening to at times.

Paul Graham, the founder of San Francisco-based startup accelerator Y Combinator, channeled this same energy in his essay "Founder Mode" [3] summarizing a talk with AirBnB founder Brian Chesky. There are two ways to run a company: founder mode and manager mode. Business books teach you about manager mode—hire experienced people and get out of the way, stay out of the details, focus on executive tasks, etc—but it doesn't work. This book is about founder mode.

The framework I propose here revolves around two basic principles. The first principle is that you—the founder—have to build your company around yourself. Build your company to your own specifications and nobody else's, so that you can maximally leverage your unique strengths. The second principle is that you have to optimize every aspect of your organization to enable quick decision making and rapid changes in direction. Only then can you experiment your way through the vast uncertainty in order to achieve your vision.

This book is organized into three parts. Part 1 focuses on you. It highlights some core questions you need to answer about yourself, preferably before even starting your company. Part 2 focuses on hiring others. It presents some practical methods for finding the "right people" for your startup, including how to find the right investors. Finally, Part 3 describes how to execute. It describes some basic principles for operating your startup to maximize speed.

---

3. https://paulgraham.com/foundermode.html

Part One
Preparing Yourself

For what is a man, what has he got?
If not himself, then he has naught
To say the things he truly feels
And not the words of one who kneels
The record shows I took the blows
And did it my way
Yes, it was my way

Frank Sinatra

1. What do you want to achieve?

If you want to create a world-changing company, then you will need an incredibly ambitious vision. Your current vision is almost certainly not big enough. Most of the first time founders I've met in the past few years have started with visions that are too small, myself included. This is because most founders start by coming up with an idea for a product or technology that they believe can solve a real world problem, or at least they believe it will be able to solve that problem after a couple years of research and development. Few people start with an idea so big that it seems nearly impossible to achieve, but they should.

Many founders start with a vision that looks something like, "Customers have such and such problem which causes such and such pain. Our new product/technology solves this problem and reduces their pain by X%. We believe they'll pay such and such money for it". If they've been indoctrinated with the MBA disease they may even try to write out a business plan for their startup! For example, at Unlearn.AI we started with a vision like, "Pharmaceutical companies have to run large, expensive clinical trials in which they pay $100,000 per enrolled participant, but half of those participants are usually given a placebo. We can use artificial intelligence to create digital twins of these participants that predict how their disease would progress if they got a placebo, thereby reducing the need for real participants to get placebos in clinical trials. We believe biopharma companies will pay us a substantial fraction of the cost that would otherwise go to enrolling those patients in the placebo group, because the time savings from being able to run smaller studies is more valuable if they can get their drug to market sooner." That sounds great! There's a clear need for this, with a large monetary value attached to it, and although it was difficult we believed we could solve this problem with a few years of research and development.

But why stop with the achievable vision? If we could use artificial intelligence to create digital twins of patients that forecast their future health and how they respond to different treatments, couldn't we use that to improve all kinds of things in medicine, not just clinical trials? Why not imagine a world in which your doctor uses your digital twin to simulate how you'll respond to different treatments in order to select the one that's just right for you? We realized that we could articulate an even bigger vision, "We will invent the technology enabling us to create a digital twin of anyone on Earth that can forecast any aspect of their health, at any point in the future, under any available treatment, and we'll use it to completely revolutionize the practice of medicine. Our first application will be reducing the need for patients to receive placebos in clinical trials..." That's much more exciting!

Articulating a smaller vision is appealing because it may seem more realistic and achievable, whereas articulating a huge ambitious vision may seem daunting and unachievable. Starting from a gigantic vision goes against the advice that you typically would get in business school or working at a large company because it's extremely risky and there's lots of uncertainty about how to achieve it. You cannot write down a detailed and well-researched business plan that leads to the achievement of your grand vision. I strongly believe that this is actually a feature of having a gigantic vision, not a bug. In fact, if you can write down a detailed and well-researched business plan describing how your startup will achieve your vision, then that's a clear sign your vision is way too small.

There are four key reasons why it's important to articulate an enormous, nearly impossible vision for your startup.

First, no matter how big or small your vision is, you're still going to encounter haters, doubters, and naysayers galore. People love to hate on anyone trying to do something new. So-called experts in the field will tell you it can't be done. Investors will tell you that a larger company will outcompete your small startup and put you out of business. Even your parents will be worried about what will become of you if you fail. You're also going to encounter lots of real setbacks. Customers don't like your prototype so it's back to the drawing board. Your champion at a large enterprise customer leaves right before your big pitch. A customer runs out of cash and refuses to pay the bill. The first three rockets you try to send to space explode during launch. But if you can articulate a really big world changing vision that is truly meaningful to you, then you'll be able to carry on despite all the naysayers and inevitable setbacks. You need to articulate a vision that is so important to you that you're willing to go through hell to achieve it, because you'll have to. Anything less, and you'll give up.

Second, a big vision appeals to the types of hardcore employees you'll need to recruit to be successful. And, you'll need those people to work *hard*. Long hours. Late nights. Weekends at the office. Work-life balance doesn't apply to those of us who take on the job of changing the world. Moreover, they're going to have weather all the same naysayers and setbacks that you will, and you will need them to stick it out when the going gets tough. Hell, you'll need them to get going even harder when the going gets tough! And, to make matters worse, you'll almost certainly have to pay them less (at least in cash) than they could earn by working at some big tech company or hedge fund. Why would anyone do that if they aren't working towards a big vision that could change the world for the better? You need your vision to be inspiring to both yourself and others so that you're able to build a team that will run through walls to get it done.

Third, you're only tricking yourself if you think you know the right steps to achieve a smaller vision. The truth is, you're going to have to pivot frequently even if you're going after something small. The problem is, you can't easily pivot if you've given yourself a narrow space to work in. By choosing a large vision, you provide yourself with lots of opportunities to learn about what will work, and what won't, without sacrificing your vision. For example, we could have articulated a narrow vision for Unlearn.AI like "Our vision is to replace the placebo groups in phase 3 clinical trials with simulated placebo groups derived from participants' digital twins, so that all of the participants in the study can get access to the experimental treatment." Although that sounds like a compelling vision, we would have immediately run into insurmountable regulatory problems. Then what? We would have had to either change the vision or shut down the company. That vision statement is too narrow, too prescribed, and doesn't leave any room for pivoting on the product or business strategy without abandoning the vision. By contrast, consider a vision statement like "Our vision is to invent a technology that will enable us to create a digital twin of anyone on Earth and use it to revolutionize the practice of medicine." This vision statement is so broad that there are many potential pathways to achieving it. We haven't specified what the specific technology is, or even what specific use cases we'll pursue to revolutionize medicine. We haven't specified the details. A big vision gives you a guiding principle that you never have to compromise on, while allowing you to remain flexible on the details about how to achieve it so that you have the necessary room to learn from your experiments.

Finally, a big vision is more appealing to investors because it provides them with an opportunity for big returns, and only the big returns matter. Startups are experiments in building big businesses. As a result, only a few startups in a venture portfolio go on to make money. In order for the investor to generate returns for themselves and their limited partners, they need the startups that win to win big. A simple rule of thumb that many investors use is to look for companies that could return the fund if they are successful. Here's an example. Suppose an investor has a $100M venture fund. They invest $4M into your seed round at a $20M post money valuation. Thus, they own a 20% stake in your company. As your company grows, you raise additional rounds of venture financing and your seed investor gets diluted so they end up owning 10% of your company. In order for your company to "return the fund" their 10% stake must be worth the original size of their fund—$100M in this case—which means your company must exit at a $1B valuation. Think about that for a second! A venture investor will only want to invest $4M in your seed round if they think your company could be worth $1B! If you are pitching to investors with a $500M fund, they will be asking if your company could be worth at least $5B. Venture capital investors want home runs, grand slams, they don't want singles or doubles. The fact is, your vision needs to be huge to attract capital from top tier investors.

To come up with your vision, I recommend starting from your initial idea for a product and then trying to expand upon it. Usually, founders have an idea for an initial product that addresses a small part of a much larger problem. You need to figure out what that much larger problem is. For example, clinical trials are just one part of the pharmaceutical industry, and the pharmaceutical industry is just one part of the healthcare industry. Roughly $100B is spent on clinical trials each year, but that is a very small part of the roughly $10T that is spent on healthcare each year. Therefore, if my initial vision is to use artificial intelligence to solve clinical trials, my expanded vision would be to use artificial intelligence to solve medicine.

Once you have this idea for your big vision, it's helpful to create three versions of it. The first version is a 10 second soundbite, the second version is an elevator pitch that should take around 1 minute, and the third version is a more detailed story of why you want to go after this big problem and how you think you can solve it that should take around 10 minutes.

This part of the process is intimidating, I'll admit. Most people balk at the audacity of articulating such a big vision. But the hard truth is, most startups fail. If you're going to take the risk, with the odds stacked against you, at least make sure it's a risk worth taking. Set your sights high.

2. What are you uniquely good at?

One of the worst pieces of advice that I got when I was CEO was to focus only on doing the executive business jobs that a CEO typically does. To focus on the traditional responsibilities of a CEO, which include managing the overall operations, financial health, and strategic direction of the company. This advice stems from the mistaken belief that there is a well defined role called a Chief Executive Officer and that the responsibilities of that role are roughly the same across different companies. But you are a founder. There is nothing forcing you to follow some outdated conventions just because that's how things are done at other legacy companies; you can define your role and the roles of other leaders at your company however you want. This is your company. You should structure it so that it works for you instead of against you.

Even at large legacy companies, different people approach the CEO role in different ways because they have different personalities, skill sets, and interests. For example, Steve Jobs focused on designing insanely great products and telling compelling narratives about what Apple stood for, whereas Tim Cook has focused more on exceptional execution and operational excellence. Steve Jobs launched insanely great products, and Tim Cook made those products insanely profitable. Apple hasn't launched any successful new product lines since Steve Jobs died, but their stock price is way up under Tim Cook's leadership. Some CEOs are internal facing and focus on developing the company culture or driving execution, while others are external facing and focus more on public relations, sales, or corporate development. Some, like Elon Musk, get extremely hands-on with product and engineering teams, whereas others like Satya Nadella of Microsoft are known as hands-off leaders who set an overall direction and let their teams figure out how to get there. These are examples of CEOs focusing on areas in which they have a comparative advantage, which is what you should do too.

My theory of leadership is based on the principle of comparative advantage. Comparative advantage is a concept from economics that says that even if one person, company, or country can produce everything more efficiently than others (that is, they have an absolute advantage), they still benefit from specializing in the area in which they have the lowest opportunity cost.

To illustrate the general concept, imagine two friends, Alice and Bob. They both can bake cookies and make lemonade, but Alice is much faster at both baking cookies and making lemonade than Bob. In fact, Alice can either bake 10 cookies in an hour or she can make 5 cups of lemonade in an hour. Bob, by contrast, can either bake 4 cookies in an hour or make 4 cups of lemonade in an hour. As a result, each hour Alice spends making lemonade means she gives up the chance to bake 10 cookies, whereas each hour Bob spends making lemonade only costs him 4 cookies. Even though Alice is better at both, Bob gives up fewer cookies to make lemonade than Alice does, so Bob has a comparative advantage in making lemonade. Alice, who gives up a lot of cookie-making time to make lemonade, has a comparative advantage in baking cookies. So, instead of each person doing both tasks, Alice should focus on baking cookies (her strength), and Bob should focus on making lemonade (his strength). Then they can trade, and both will end up with more cookies and lemonade than if they tried to do both tasks themselves.

According to the principle of comparative advantage, you should spend more time on areas in which you perform well relative to others, and spend less time on areas in which you perform poorly relative to others. What are you really good at, that others are really bad at? Being an effective leader requires you to be self-aware about your strengths and weaknesses. You should not spend much time as a founder/CEO trying to get better at things you're not good at or don't enjoy doing. Please read that sentence again, because it says the opposite of so much advice we get throughout our lives. Trying to bring up your areas of weakness is a complete waste of your time, energy, and talents. It is bad for you, because you will hate doing it, and it is terrible for your company because it violates a fundamental principle of economics! Your company will be much better off if you lean further into the things you're already relatively good at, and then hire people with complementary skills to whom you can delegate the things you are relatively bad at.

Before you bring on even a single other person into your company, including a co-founder, you need to spend a substantial amount of time trying to figure out what you are uniquely good at. If you've already started your company and have co-founders or colleagues, you should get on this immediately. Reach out to former colleagues and mentors, or pull up performance reviews from previous jobs, and see what they say.

Technically, you can't talk about your areas of comparative advantage without having someone to compare to. But, I'm a physicist not an economist. Approximate is good enough. I'm just trying to get at the spirit of the thing, and to come up with a useful framework that founders can apply to figure out which areas of their startup they should focus on personally.

In general, I think that most people should try to structure their roles around their areas of comparative advantage. That is, I think this principle should apply beyond startups and beyond the role of the founder and CEO. However, it works particularly well for founder/CEOs because they have the authority to define their role and to hire anyone they need, and it's better for them to use their time to hire someone than learning to fill the gaps themselves.

Here are two exercises you can try to figure out which areas to focus on.

The first exercise is based on a simple algorithm called a double sort. As an aside, I love the double sort algorithm because it's a simple way to rank choices that accounts for multiple attributes of each choice. It's a useful heuristic for solving many ranked choice problems. In this case, you want to focus on problems that are important to your business, that you enjoy doing, and that are areas of relative strength.

To start, write down a list of different areas that you could spend time on at your startup. Next, rank these areas by how important you think they are for your business. So, if you have written down ten areas, the most important area gets a rank of 1 and the least important area gets a rank of 10. Next, rank the areas by how much you enjoy doing them. Again, the area you most enjoy working on gets a rank of 1 and the area you least enjoy working on gets a rank of 10. Then, rank the areas by how good you are at them relative (in your estimation) to someone else who you could hire to focus on that area. If you already have co-founders, you could also rank your skill relative to them. Thus, the area in which you think you are best at gets a rank of 1 and the area in which you think you are worst at gets a rank of 10. Finally, add these ranks together to get a score for each choice. You should focus on the areas with the lowest scores.

I'll use myself as an example. I"ll consider the case of an early stage tech startup, and have listed 10 potential areas of focus along with how I would rank them according to importance, enjoyment, and relative skill. The table is ordered by total score.

Areas	Importance	Enjoyment	Relative Skill	Total Score
Vision.	1	2	2	5
Research and development.	4	1	3	8
Startup culture.	2	7	1	10
Product.	3	5	4	12
Engineering.	5	3	5	13
Marketing.	7	4	6	17
Sales.	8	6	7	21
Management.	6	8	8	22
Operations.	9	9	9	27
Finance.	10	10	10	30

Note that how you should rank these areas by importance depends both on what your startup does, and what stage it's at. For example, finance is not a very important function at an early stage startup that's just been founded, but is a very important function at a later stage company that's getting ready to go public. Thus, the importance ranks could change from one year to the next, but your enjoyment and relative skills ranks should generally not change over time.

Based on this double sort exercise, I should spend the majority of my time refining and evangelizing the vision for my startup, getting hands on in R&D, and working to create a relentless startup culture. I should try to delegate everything else. Of course, there could be nobody else to delegate these areas to at a very early stage startup, in which case I would try to find co-founders to cover these other areas or to hire people once my startup had sufficient resources.

Notice that this framework tries to balance how important the area is to the business, with how much enjoyment you get out of it, and how good at it you are. For example, I believe that creating a strong startup culture (i.e., a culture that is face paced, decisive, bold, agile, resilient, etc) is an extremely important ingredient for success, second only to the company's vision. I also think that I'm much better at this than others because most people I've encountered seem to think that "culture = fun" when the reality is "culture = performance;" the average employee in Silicon Valley will actually move your company's culture in the wrong direction. However, I don't actually enjoy doing the work of creating this type of culture very much because it constantly brings me into conflict with everyone around me—it's a frustrating job. Nevertheless, it's very important to the company and I'm quite good at it so it's something I should focus on even if I find it frustrating.

Research and development, on the other hand, is fourth on the list in terms of importance. Traditionally, a CEO is not directly involved in R&D. But I'm a physicist! R&D is the thing that I get maximum enjoyment out of at work. And, I think I'm generally really good at inventing stuff. So, even though it's not on the usual CEO areas of responsibility, it would be on mine.

An alternative framework is based on the number one tool of business school, the 2x2 matrix. Place things you are relatively bad to the left along the horizontal axis, and things you are relatively good at the right along the horizontal axis. Place things you think others who you could hire are relatively good at to the bottom of the vertical axis, and place things you think others are relatively bad at to the top of the vertical axis. Your areas of advantage will be the things that fall in the top right.

Avoid Entirely Things you are relatively bad at, that others are also relatively bad at.	Focus Things you are relatively good at that others are relatively bad at.
Delegate Things you are relatively bad at, that others are relatively good at.	Delegate Things you are relatively good at, but others are relatively good at too.

To be a bit more concrete, I'll use myself as an example. For years, I've described myself as having only three key skills: (i) creating and evangelizing a vision, (ii) research and development, and (iii) fostering a startup culture. That is, these are the three areas in which I believe I have a comparative advantage; they are the things that belong in the top right quadrant of my 2x2 matrix. Here's an example of what my 2x2 matrix might look like.

Avoid Entirely (depends on business)	Focus Startup culture. Vision. Research and Development.
Delegate Sales. Management. Operations. Finance.	Delegate Product. Engineering. Marketing.

Essentially, I think I'm pretty good at fostering a startup culture, at creating a vision, and at R&D and I don't think it would be easy to hire someone who could do these tasks as well as I could. While I also think I'm pretty good at product, engineering, and marketing, I think it's generally pretty easy to find someone who can do those tasks as well, or better than I can. Therefore, I should delegate those areas even though I think I'm pretty good at them. Then, there are areas like sales, management, operations, and finance that I know little about, and should definitely delegate.

Each of these frameworks is just a heuristic, a tool for helping to think through which areas of your business you'd like to focus on as the founder and CEO. It's not an exact science. I suggest trying out both frameworks, and seeing what makes most sense for you.

It turns out that the results of my analyses align pretty well with a particular archetype of CEO called an "Inventor CEO", but this took me years to realize. The reason it took me so long to realize this isn't because of a lack of self-awareness, it's because I didn't realize such a thing existed (Inventor CEOs are quite rare, even within the technology sector only about 1-in-10 CEOs is an active inventor [1]). Even worse, lots of the people around me kept telling me to focus on the bottom left quadrant instead of the things I should have been focusing on in the top right quadrant. Eventually, however, I happened across some academic literature on the topic of Inventor CEOs. In the literature, an Inventor CEO is usually defined as an acting CEO who is listed as a primary inventor on one or more

---

1. https://www.sciencedirect.com/science/article/abs/pii/
S0304405X19301667

of a company's patents. That definition makes it easy for researchers because it's based on publicly available information, but it's a bit narrow in my opinion because it fails to capture other invention-like activities that one can work on, including engineering and product design, that aren't typically reflected in patent applications.

The following characteristics are common attributes of Inventor CEOs.

- Technical Expertise: They usually have a deep understanding of the technical aspects of their company's products or services. This could be in fields like artificial intelligence, biotechnology, or engineering.
- Innovation-Driven: Their approach to leadership is often characterized by a focus on innovation. They might actively participate in research and development activities, contribute to patents, or be involved in designing new products.
- Visionary Leadership: Inventor CEOs are often visionaries who can see how technological advancements can be translated into successful business models. They tend to be forward-thinking and adept at identifying future trends and opportunities.
- Hands-On Approach: Unlike CEOs who primarily focus on managerial and administrative responsibilities, Inventor CEOs are often more hands-on in the creative and developmental aspects of their company's products or technologies.

Now that I understand my areas of comparative advantage, I can define the CEO role around them. If I am taking on a new role as a founder/CEO, then the CEO role at my new company would be defined as setting and owning the vision, leading external evangelism and fundraising, driving the research and development strategy, and getting hands-on in the development of the company's products and technologies. Now that I have defined my role as the founder/CEO, I can think about what other roles would be needed to complement my areas of focus and ensure we have all of the necessary expertise to be successful. For example, I would need someone in operations to make the trains run on time, someone in finance to make sure we understand our business, someone in human resources to focus on people management, someone in sales and marketing to focus on distribution, someone in product management or design to help create great products, and an engineering leader to focus on computing and software engineering. At a small startup, I would probably aim to bring on people in product and engineering first, and then I'd fill the other roles as needed. At a later stage company, I'd want to have someone on my leadership team covering each of these areas.

In summary, after you've defined your big, world changing vision you should take some time to reflect on your areas of relative strength. Then, throw out the textbook definition of what a CEO does and just define the role as focusing on your particular areas of comparative advantage. Finally, figure out what gaps remain for your business and define roles that fill those gaps. I recommend writing specific descriptions of these roles and responsibilities, including a description of the responsibilities you're assigning to yourself as CEO, so that there's no uncertainty about what you'll be focusing on and what you'll be delegating. As you grow, you'll undoubtedly meet investors and executives who'll tell you to change your focus, and to start doing more "CEO things", but you'll be okay if you just tell those people to go pound sand.

3. What's your natural working style?

I've met all types of founders over the years. People who are relatively quiet and contemplative, people who are outgoing and bubbly, and people who are intense warriors. The truth is, aspects of your personality and character are even more important for defining your leadership style than your knowledge and skills. It's crucially important that you understand your working style, and that you write it down, preferably before you bring on any co-founders or employees. That way, you can form your company's culture around your working style to make sure that it works for you. Whatever you do, do not change your style to accommodate a different style from one of your co-founders or employees. It's your company, and if they don't fit within your style then the relationship isn't going to work out. Personality conflicts are common in life, and it's better to accept that as a fact and part ways than to keep trying to work together in a downward spiral that will inevitably lead to burnout.

I've generally found that a person's working style is influenced by a combination of their personality traits and their values. For example, a person who is extroverted will probably have a different working style than a person who is introverted. Likewise, a person who values social impact will probably have a different working style than a person who values financial returns. As a general rule, people usually find it easiest to get along with others who share similar personality traits and values. Therefore, I believe you want a startup to be made of a group of people with a diversity of skills, complementary personalities, and strongly aligned values.

The first step down this road is understanding what your skills, personality traits, and values actually are. You thought about your skills in the last chapter, and you'll think about your values in the next one. In this chapter, your goal is to craft a simple description of your personality that you think is reasonably accurate, and that you can share with potential colleagues so that they can judge if they think they'd be a good fit for you. I'll use myself as an example, and will walk through a process to draft such a description.

As an example, here's a description of my personality.

"I'm not the type to sit back and let things just happen to me. I shape the world around me and take control of outcomes—I'm driven by this deep, unshakable belief that, if something's going to get done, I'm the one who's going to do it.

I'm relentless. I'm not here to tiptoe around comfort zones, mine or anyone else's. I go after big, bold ideas, the kind that make people squirm a little because they can't quite wrap their heads around them. If it's complex, uncharted, or supposedly "impossible," I'm diving into the deep end. I'm driven by the thrill of taking things apart, seeing how they work, and pushing them beyond their limits—because, let's be real, pushing boundaries is where the magic happens. I value intuition as much as data, because data always comes from the past and can only get you what you've already got; it takes creativity to make something new.

I feel a deep seated need to move fast. And, I'm easily frustrated when I think the people around me are moving too slowly, particularly when they can't just make a goddamned decision. When I'm with people, I don't sugarcoat, and I don't dance around issues. I speak my mind, get to the heart of things, and drive us forward. I thrive in environments that let me shake things up, throw my weight behind big ideas, and make shit happen. If it means breaking convention or ruffling feathers, so be it. Some people don't like working with me because they think I'm too intense, but others realize that I'm a passionate, high agency, goal oriented person who cares deeply about doing great work and making the world better. This passion is contagious for the right people. I'm here to leave a mark, and I'm not waiting around for permission.

Do I get anxious? Of course. Stressed out sometimes? You bet. But I get over it quickly. Stress and obstacles are fuel, plain and simple. When the going gets tough, the tough get going.

I've got a passion for new ideas and a restlessness that drives me to leave a mark. If there's an obstacle, I'll bulldoze through it. If there's a limit, I'm going to push past it. I'm an unstoppable force. I'm not here to blend in or go along quietly. I'm here to break ground, move fast, and make damn sure people feel the impact of what I do."

Some people find discussion of personality types or traits to be a bit woo-woo. In fact, I think this is actually an indicator of a particular personality type. In my experience, however, personality traits can provide a helpful language for framing discussions around working styles. In addition, I've had a few different executive coaches over the years and the first thing every one of them did was give personality tests to me and my teammates. You might as well get it out of the way now, and it'll be a lot less expensive this way.

In principle, if you are extremely self aware, then you may be able to craft a description of your personality like the one above from scratch. Most people are not that self aware. Using a personality assessment can help get around that problem, but it's important to keep in mind that personality tests are still self-assessments. If you don't answer honestly, then you'll be lying to both yourself and your future colleagues, and setting yourself up for a lot of pain, suffering, and failure. There are a few popular tools for assessing personality, but to keep the amount of woo-woo-ness to a minimum I'll focus on Big Five personality traits because they are the most widely studied in the psychometric literature. The Big Five personality traits are Openness, Conscientiousness, Extraversion, Agreeableness, and Neuroticism. [1] Sometimes these are abbreviated as

---

1. https://www.psychologytoday.com/us/basics/big-5-personality-traits

OCEAN.

Openness refers to a person's willingness to engage with new ideas, experiences, and creative pursuits. It reflects intellectual curiosity, imagination, and a preference for novelty. People high in openness tend to be creative, curious, and open-minded. They enjoy exploring new ideas, art, and cultures, and often seek out unconventional experiences. Those low in openness tend to prefer routine, familiarity, and traditional thinking. They may be more practical and less interested in abstract or imaginative pursuits.

Conscientiousness is the trait that reflects a person's degree of organization, self-discipline, and reliability. It involves goal-oriented behaviors, careful planning, and a strong sense of duty. Individuals high in conscientiousness are organized, reliable, and hard-working. They are often seen as disciplined, responsible, and detail-oriented. People low in conscientiousness may be more spontaneous, less organized, and less focused on long-term goals. They might be more comfortable with flexibility and may sometimes struggle with follow-through.

Extraversion reflects the extent to which a person is outgoing, sociable, and energized by interacting with others. It also captures traits like assertiveness, excitement-seeking, and a preference for stimulating environments. People who score high in extraversion are typically outgoing, talkative, and enjoy being around others. They tend to be energetic, assertive, and thrive in social situations. Those low in extraversion (introverts) tend to prefer quieter, solitary activities. They are often more reserved, reflective, and get their energy from time spent alone or in small, close-knit groups.

Agreeableness is the trait that measures a person's tendency to be compassionate, cooperative, and empathetic toward others. It reflects how well someone gets along with others and their orientation toward social harmony. Highly agreeable individuals are often warm, empathetic, and cooperative. They are inclined to trust others, avoid conflict, and prioritize relationships and kindness. People with low agreeableness tend to be more skeptical, competitive, and sometimes more direct or blunt. They may prioritize their own needs over maintaining harmony in social situations.

Neuroticism refers to a person's tendency to experience negative emotions such as anxiety, moodiness, and emotional instability. It reflects how emotionally reactive and vulnerable to stress someone is. People who score high in neuroticism are more likely to experience anxiety, stress, and emotional volatility. They may be more sensitive to criticism or challenges and tend to worry more about negative outcomes. Individuals with low neuroticism tend to be emotionally stable, calm, and less prone to experiencing negative emotions. They are generally more resilient to stress and less likely to be overwhelmed by challenges.

These personality traits will have a strong impact on your leadership and working styles, whether you want them to, are aware of it, or not. In my opinion, it's much better to be aware of it and to make your future co-founders and colleagues aware of it too. Therefore, I suggest going online and taking a Big Five personality test or two (there's lots of them available). You can also ask a large language model such as ChatGPT to help you interpret your results and what they may mean for your working style.

Here's the recipe I used to write my personality description.

First, I took a Big Five personality test online.[2] I took the test twice a few weeks apart to get a rough estimate for the test-retest error, which was honestly lower than I expected, but you don't have to do that. My scores were: Openness (85/90), Conscientiousness (48/54), Extraversion (73/77), Agreeableness (6/10), and Neuroticism (50/46). I don't know how much the numbers really matter, and it's simpler to translate these into something like high (greater than or equal to 75), medium (between 25 and 75), or low (less than or equal to 25). This means I have High Openness, Medium Conscientiousness, High Extraversion, Low Agreeableness, and Medium Neuroticism.

I find these broader personality traits a bit hard to interpret; I'm not a psychologist after all. So, I used a large language model to help interpret these scores.

"Openness (Score: 85): A high score here indicates that you're highly imaginative, creative, and curious. You enjoy exploring new ideas and seeking out new experiences. This aligns with your passion for big, bold ideas and pushing boundaries.

Conscientiousness (Score: 48): An average score suggests you

----

2. https://www.truity.com/test/big-five-personality-test

strike a balance between being organized and valuing flexibility. You're reliable when needed but also appreciate spontaneity and aren't overly rigid in your planning. This fits with your preference for moving fast and not getting bogged down by excessive structure.

Extraversion (Score: 73): A high score means you're outgoing, energetic, and sociable. You thrive in social situations, enjoy being around others, and are enthusiastic and assertive. This matches your direct communication style and your ability to energize those around you.

Agreeableness (Score: 6): A low score indicates you may be less concerned with social harmony and more focused on your own goals. You're likely to be direct, assertive, and possibly more critical in your interactions. This resonates with your candid approach and willingness to ruffle feathers to get things done.

Neuroticism (Score: 50): An average score suggests you're generally emotionally stable but may experience occasional stress or negative emotions. You handle pressure reasonably well and bounce back from setbacks, which aligns with your acknowledgment of feeling stress but using it as fuel."

That's pretty useful and does a good job describing my general characteristics; at least, that's how I perceive myself. Interestingly, people who only know me socially are sometimes surprised that I have high extroversion because it's coupled with low agreeableness; I don't have the bubbly personality commonly associated with an extrovert, but nevertheless feel right at home on stage talking in front of thousands of people. The problem with these descriptions, however, is that not everyone is going to be familiar with the Big Five personality traits. So, referring back to them in your summary isn't very useful. It's also boring. So, I asked a language model to spice it up a bit. I used the following prompt:

"My Big Five personality traits are: High Openness (85/90), Moderate Conscientiousness (48/54), High Extraversion (73/77), Low Agreeableness (6/10), and Moderate Neuroticism (50/46). I took the test twice a few weeks apart to get some idea for the test-retest error, and give both scores for each dimension. Please use these data to write a description of my personality that would make sense to someone who doesn't know anything about the Big Five personality traits. That is, just use plain language and examples rather than referring to the traits or my test results directly. Your description should be colorful and memorable, it should impact the reader. Make it three paragraphs. Please write the description in the first person. Don't worry about sounding professional. Feel free to use profanity if you think I would."

Then I simply edited the result to come up with the description of my personality from the beginning of the chapter.

Now, if I follow up to ask the large language model how these personality traits may translate to a preferred working environment. Here's what it said.

"I thrive in an environment that's as fast-paced and dynamic as I am. Put me in a place where big ideas aren't just welcomed—they're the lifeblood of the operation. I need the freedom to move quickly, take risks, and shake things up without getting tangled in bureaucratic bullshit or red tape. Let's cut the endless meetings and get straight to making things happen.

I want to be surrounded by passionate, high-agency people who aren't afraid to roll up their sleeves and dive headfirst into ambitious projects. Collaboration is key, but so is decisiveness. I can't stand when folks hem and haw over trivial details or can't make a goddamned decision. Let's trust our instincts, make the call, and keep the momentum going.

An open, transparent environment where everyone speaks their mind suits me best. I value candor over politeness—there's no time for tiptoeing around egos when we're aiming to make a real impact. Give me a team that's ready to challenge each other, push boundaries, and isn't afraid to ruffle a few feathers along the way.

Flexibility and adaptability are non-negotiables. Rigid processes and outdated rules just slow us down. If there's a better way to do something, I want the freedom to pursue it—immediately. I value intuition and creativity just as much as data and analytics. Sometimes you have to go with your gut to break new ground.

I need a workspace that's buzzing with energy—a place where challenges are seen as opportunities, and everyone is driven to leave their mark. Stagnation is the enemy. I feed off constant movement, innovation, and the relentless pursuit of excellence.

In short, I flourish in environments that embrace bold thinking, swift action, and unapologetic ambition. Let's skip the small talk and safe bets—I'm here to change the game, and I need a workplace that's ready to do the same."

This is an excellent description of my preferred working environment. I love working on creative problems, inventing new technologies and products, and *hate* the idea of doing things the same old way. I move extremely quickly, and need to be in a fast paced, results-oriented environment. I'm very comfortable public speaking and pitching to investors or customers, but I don't like networking because I can't stand small talk and am not particularly interested in meeting lots of new people unless I have a clear goal in mind. I'm extremely direct in my communication to the point of being terse, particularly when I'm unhappy about something, and I readily admit that I care vastly more about achieving results than I do about people's feelings. I like to get things done sequentially, one thing at a time, but I typically don't plan multiple steps into the future. I like doing much more than planning and generally find detailed planning to be a tedious and useless waste of time; I just do the first thing on my priority list and then decide what I should do next. I also approach problem solving more through intuition than step-by-step logic, which sometimes limits my ability to explain the reasoning behind my decisions. Lastly, I excel in bulldozing through any obstacles in my path, I try to be relentless in pursuit of my vision, but I am easily frustrated when things are moving slower than I want them to.

After reading all of the above, do you think you'd want to work with me? If the answer is "no", it won't hurt my feelings. The personality traits above are common for entrepreneurs. But, not everyone is compatible. That's why I think it's important to go through this exercise before bringing on any co-founders or employees if you can. You need to know who you are, so that you can figure out who you should work with (and who you shouldn't). In fact, you should write out a short "user guide" that describes your personality traits and your preferred working environment for future candidates—that's right, you need to give your personal user guide to all candidates before they decide to come work with you so that they can make an informed decision.

To be clear, I don't believe that a person's personality traits are good or bad. They just are. In addition, I don't think there's any strong evidence that a person's personality traits make them more or less likely to be successful as an entrepreneur. So, the purpose of this exercise isn't to figure out if you have a good or bad personality, or good or bad personality traits, because there's no such thing. The goal of this exercise is simply to develop a better understanding of who you are and how you typically work, so that you can make sure your company's culture supports your preferred working style and so you can communicate this style to future co-founders and colleagues to make sure you are compatible. No matter what anyone tells you, you should never entertain the idea that you have to change your personality in order to be a successful entrepreneur or leader. It's your company, if someone doesn't like working with you then they should go work someplace else. Be you.

4. What do you value?

A person's values are the fundamental beliefs, principles, or standards that guide their behavior, decisions, and interactions with others. They represent what is most important to you in life and serve as a compass for your actions and choices. Values are deeply held convictions about what is right, important, or desirable, influencing how you prioritize your time, energy, and resources. Examples of common personal values include integrity, which involves valuing honesty and consistency in actions and words; innovation, which prioritizes creativity and the development of new ideas; achievement, meaning striving for excellence and accomplishment; compassion, characterized by caring for others and showing empathy; efficiency, valuing productivity and the effective use of resources; freedom, which prioritizes autonomy and the ability to make one's own choices; collaboration, valuing teamwork and collective effort; and learning, the pursuit of knowledge and personal growth.

Figuring out your values is important before starting your company for many reasons. First and foremost, it will help you make sure that you use your startup to pursue something that truly matters to you. Second, communicating your values to potential teammates can help you find like-minded people who share those values. If you can find people who share your values, and fit with your personality and your preferred working environment, then you can find life-long colleagues who'll stick with you through thick and thin. On the other hand, it can be extremely difficult working with people who share a very different set of values from your own, particularly in a high pressure and rapidly changing environment like a startup.

One area that's often neglected when people talk about values is aesthetics. Aesthetics, broadly speaking, are the set of principles someone uses to define what they like or dislike. The term is often associated specifically with the appreciation of art or beauty, but I think aesthetic principles apply much more broadly than that. They are the (often unconscious and implicit) principles that give you the initial impression of something, the impression that you like or dislike something from your first glance at it. For example, for a theoretical physicist like myself aesthetics extends to the elegance of theories, the simplicity of equations, and the inherent symmetry of many laws of nature.

Every great company is built around a sense of aesthetics, whether the founder is aware of it or not. For example, let's contrast the aesthetic principles expressed by Steve Jobs at Apple and Bill Gates at Microsoft. Steve Jobs was famous for his obsession with simplicity, elegance, and intuitive design.

He believed that products should offer seamless integration of form and function, resulting in minimalist designs that are both visually appealing and user-friendly. In contrast, Bill Gates prioritized practicality and widespread accessibility. Under his leadership, Microsoft's focus was on functionality and utility, aiming to create versatile software tools that could enhance productivity for a broad audience. Gates's aesthetic principles leaned towards straightforward, no-frills designs that emphasized reliability and efficiency over visual flair. Steve Jobs famously said, "The problem with Microsoft is they just have no taste." But that's not really true. Utilitarian aesthetics is, indeed, a type of aesthetics. Bill Gates just had a different set of values from Steve Jobs, and this manifested in Microsoft expressing a different sense of aesthetics.

In most aspects of life, it's fine to leave your core values and aesthetic principles implicit; especially if you're working alone. The problem arises when you start to bring other people into the creative process, as you will when you bring on co-founders or begin to hire employees at your startup. If you are not operating with a shared set of principles, you'll soon encounter some frustrating sources of friction. Maybe you don't like the new website design proposed by your marketing team. Or, perhaps your engineers are arguing about the architecture of a new software library. Or, perhaps your product team starts pushing through any feature requested by your users, even if your varying users have conflicting desires. The lack of a shared set of aesthetic principles leads to the development of Frankenstein products, with pieces stitched together from multiple people's preferences. Even your definition of success for your startup can differ fundamentally from your colleagues if you share different values. These differences can lead to arguments that are difficult to resolve because they revolve around unstated principles of taste rather than logic.

So, in order to avoid these issues, an additional piece of preparatory work I suggest you do is write down a short description of the principles that describe your core values and your personal sense of aesthetics. Unfortunately, much like one's personality traits, it's difficult to simply articulate your core principles. Such things are often only semi-conscious. Even worse, there aren't widely used psychometric assessments for such things. Therefore, I've come up with a list of 15 questions to help guide you. I'll go through them below, providing my answers as an example.

Core Values

1. Reflect on a moment when you felt extremely satisfied or proud of something you accomplished. What was it, and what aspects contributed to that feeling?

This question helps identify what brings you fulfillment and the values associated with those accomplishments (e.g., achievement, impact, creativity).

My Answer: I am never extremely satisfied. There is always something that I could have done better, always more to accomplish.

2. Think about a time when you were frustrated or unhappy with a situation at work or in life. What specific factors caused those feelings?

This reveals what you find intolerable or incompatible with your values (e.g., inefficiency, lack of integrity, rigidity).

My Answer: I get frustrated when I've made up my mind about what direction to go, but the people on my team get stuck in indecision. I'd rather flip a coin and adjust course as necessary than sit around and endlessly debate what to do.

3. What activities or tasks make you lose track of time because you're so engaged in them? What do these activities have in common?

Understanding this can highlight your passions and the values they represent (e.g., innovation, problem-solving, helping others).

My Answer: Thinking about science and deriving equations, programming, writing, and building things (i.e., physical things, like construction projections). All these activities involve deeply engaging in creative problem-solving to build or create something new, whether conceptually or physically.

4. Who are three people you deeply admire (they can be people you know personally or public figures), and what qualities do they embody that resonate with you?

This helps you identify values you aspire to, such as leadership, courage, or compassion.

My Answer: Arnold Schwarzenegger once said "The worst thing I could be is just like everyone else. I'd hate that." Elon Musk embodies the spirit of innovation, relentless drive, and belief in the nearly impossible. Richard Feynman embodied intellectual curiosity, the use of plain language, and disrespect for authority. Interestingly, all three of these people had some flaws, but I can accept the good with the bad.

5. When faced with a difficult decision, what criteria do you usually consider most important?

This uncovers your decision-making priorities and underlying values (e.g., ethical considerations, long-term impact, personal growth).

My Answer: If there are ethical considerations or something like that, then it isn't a difficult decision. Decisions with clear and large consequences are easy to make. Difficult decisions are ones where the consequences are unclear, in which case I trust my gut instinct.

6. Describe a situation where you stood up for something you believed in, even if it was unpopular or risky. What motivated you to do so?

This reveals values you're willing to defend, such as justice, honesty, or innovation.

My Answer: Two things come to mind from my first startup. One is the pursuit of rapid technological innovation in medical research, which is traditionally a very conservative field. The second is the need for relentlessness and intensity when building a startup, that there is no such thing as "work/life balance" for people trying to change the world.

7. What are three things you absolutely cannot tolerate in a professional or personal setting?

Identifying these deal-breakers highlights values that are non-negotiable for you (e.g., dishonesty, disrespect, complacency).

My Answer: Dishonesty and lying is a clear number one. A second is being closed-minded, preventing people from trying new things. A third is lacking courage, particularly when it comes to making difficult decisions or taking action.

8. What types of problems are you naturally drawn to solving, and why do they interest you?

This sheds light on your innate interests and the values they represent (e.g., challenge, creativity, service).

My Answer: I like problems that seem incredibly challenging, preferably people tell me they are nearly impossible, problems that have the potential to change the course of humanity if we can solve them, and problems that require creativity.

9. How do you typically respond to failure or setbacks? Can you provide an example?

Your response can reveal values like resilience, learning, and adaptability.

My Answer: When the going gets tough, the tough get going! I will bulldoze any obstacle put in front of me if that's what's required to achieve my mission.

10. If you could be remembered for one thing after you're gone, what would you want it to be, and why?

This question helps you articulate your ultimate aspirations and core values (e.g., making a difference, pioneering change, kindness).

My Answer: This is a difficult choice between innovation and relentlessness. I suppose I would choose innovation over relentlessness, but it's close.

Aesthetic Principles

1. What is the single most important quality you value in any design (whether it's a product, theory, or artwork)?

This question helps identify the primary aesthetic principle that resonates with you, such as simplicity, functionality, or innovation.

My Answer: I appreciate things that make complex ideas more intuitive and straightforward. To paraphrase Albert Einstein— everything should be made as simple as possible, but not simpler.

2. When you encounter a design you dislike, what's typically the reason?

This reveals the design elements or principles that you find unappealing, highlighting your aesthetic dislikes and possible deal-breakers.

My Answer: I typically dislike things that try to do too much, or serve too many different types of audiences, and end up cluttered and unnecessarily complicated as a result.

3. How do you balance form and function? Do you lean more toward visual appeal or practical effectiveness?

This explores your prioritization between aesthetics and utility, shedding light on how you integrate both in your preferences.

My Answer: If something doesn't work, then I don't like it. Therefore, functionality is the most important thing. But I think the creator should take a stance about which type of functionality is important, and which is not important, and express those opinions through a minimalist design. What you leave out of something is just as important as what you put in.

4. What feeling or experience do you want a design to evoke in its audience or users?

This uncovers the emotional or experiential impact you value in designs, such as inspiration, clarity, or curiosity.

My Answer: I want things to evoke a sense of immediate understanding while also making the audience intrigued to dive in and learn more. So, clarity and curiosity.

5. Do you value innovation over tradition, or vice versa, in design?

This question helps determine your stance on creativity versus conventional approaches within aesthetics.

My Answer: Without question, I value innovation over tradition. The ultimate form of creativity is to come up with something that is simultaneously novel, simple, and useful.

———

Take some time to think through how you would answer these questions. If you want, you could include these questions and your answers directly in your user guide along with the description of your personality and preferred working environment. Alternatively, you could use a language model to extract your core principles from your answers and write them up in a couple of paragraphs as below:

"My core values center on a relentless drive and ambition. I'm never fully satisfied and always believe there's more to accomplish. Drawn to incredibly challenging problems that can change humanity, I value innovation over tradition and aim to pioneer impactful solutions. Action and decisiveness are crucial to me; I become frustrated with indecision and prefer making bold choices and adjusting as necessary. Integrity and honesty are non-negotiable. I value open-mindedness and the courage to try new things and make difficult decisions. When faced with obstacles, I push harder to achieve my mission, admiring individuality and those who challenge the status quo.

In terms of aesthetics, I deeply appreciate simplicity and clarity. I value designs that make complex ideas intuitive, adhering to the principle of making things as simple as possible but not simpler. Functionality is paramount; if something doesn't work, it's unacceptable regardless of visual appeal. I believe in minimalist design, recognizing that what is left out is as important as what is included. I have a strong aversion to clutter and overcomplication, preferring innovation over tradition to create something novel, simple, and useful. My aesthetic principles mirror my core values, emphasizing innovation, functionality, and the elegance of simplicity."

As a final point, it's important that you learn to recognize whether or not you like something reliably, and to get comfortable communicating this to your colleagues. It is especially helpful if you learn to identify what you specifically do or don't like about something, and to be able to communicate those specific attributes. Being able to reliably identify who you will or won't like working with is a critical skill for hiring well. And, being able to reliably identify which aspects of a product, technology, or presentation that you like or don't like, and developing the ability to clearly communicate those attributes to your colleagues, will make it much easier for your company to build great things and tell compelling narratives.

5. Who do you like working with?

Unfortunately, there are few people in this world who can get along equally well with everybody. Most of us tend to get along well with some people, and less well with others. Moreover, this can vary by context. You may enjoy hanging out with your best friend on the weekends, but wouldn't be able to stand working with them in an office for more than an hour. As an entrepreneur, you have an incredible opportunity—a luxury not afforded to many people, like those working at large companies—you get to choose the people you work with. If you choose wisely, you can create an environment you find energizing, that makes you excited to get to work and take on the world. If you choose poorly, you will create an environment that drains and frustrates you until you have nothing left.

This is the most important lesson I took away from my first stint as a startup founder and CEO, but it's not what I started out believing. In the beginning, I believed that it was most important to hire people with the right experience, skills, and knowledge, even if I didn't immediately click with those people. In fact, I remember explaining this concept to the entire company at some point; that in order to find people with the right skills and experience we would actually have to recruit people who we wouldn't be friends with, maybe even people we wouldn't like very much. But this was an incredibly stupid blunder on my part, for two reasons. First, and most importantly, it's much easier to be an effective founder and CEO if you enjoy working with your colleagues, and they enjoy working with you. Someone with specialized skills may be valuable in the short term, but how are you going to work together for the next five years if your personalities clash or you have opposite values? What happens as your company grows from 10 to 100 people if you don't get along with many of your colleagues? The CEO job is lonely enough without making it harder on yourself. The second reason not to hire for specialized skills is that it's relatively easy for someone to learn new skills, but nearly impossible for someone to learn a new attitude. There's only one conclusion to draw from this, which every founder I've met has learned eventually. Hire for attitude and teach skills.

As in previous chapters, I'll use myself as an example. It turns out that I had already been thinking about this issue myself before starting to write this book, and before going through the exercises to better understand my personality, preferred working environment, and core values. I had simply observed that I tend to work well with people if they exhibit all of the following traits:

- They are authentic and honest.

- They value innovation and think creatively.
- They are decisive and take quick, bold actions.
- They are mentally tough, and direct in communication.
- They are pragmatic and care about results rather than processes.

And that I tend to class with people if they exhibit even one of the following anti-traits:

- They are full of shit.
- They like to follow convention.
- They are overly deliberate and cautious.
- They are overly sensitive, or passive aggressive.
- They value theory or process more than results and impact.

I've met a number of people who exhibit these anti-traits who are quite successful, and some of these traits may even be assets in particular fields. For example, there are lots of jobs where being extremely deliberate and cautious is an asset, but I don't think it's an asset at a startup and it personally drives me crazy. I'd rather flip a coin than get analysis-paralysis on a decision. In addition, I've met a number of other startup founder/CEOs who I thought were full of shit, but they managed to build valuable businesses anyway. To repeat my message from the previous chapter, there's no definitive thing as a good or bad personality trait but there are things that you value in potential colleagues, so your list may be very different from mine. That's fine, the important thing is that you write them down and put them in your personal user guide.

Notice that I assess someone as likely to be a good colleague for me if they hit every single one of my positive traits, and as unlikely to be a good colleague for me if they hit even one of my anti-traits. You want this to be a strong filter. At the same time, I suggest keeping the list to five (or fewer) items; otherwise, nobody will pass through the filter and you'll be stuck all by yourself. Of course, it's also important to keep in mind that personality traits are a continuum, and there's some fuzziness in how they are assessed. You should think of each of these traits as shades of gray rather than black and white. I'll discuss some ways to make hiring for personality and culture fit a bit more objective later on in this book. For now, the goal is simply to draft a document that you can use to communicate your expectations to others.

The truth is, I couldn't have easily articulated the personality traits that make someone a good/bad fit for my natural working style when I started my first company. I probably could have told you that I prefer to work with people who are authentic and honest over people who are full of shit, but I don't think I could have told you how strongly I believe that; people who are full of shit are the worst. I could also have told you that I prefer working with people who are mentally tough and direct in communication over those who are sensitive or passive-aggressive. I like stereotypical East Coast personalities. But, I probably wouldn't have articulated the other three traits. I just didn't have enough life experience at the time. And I was in my early 30s, so I imagine this could be even more difficult for a founder coming straight out of college.

You can use your personality profile to gain some insights into the types of people you may work well with, and those you may clash with. You should write some thoughts about this in your personal user guide that you give to potential co-founders and job candidates. In addition, these traits, along with your preferred working environment and values, will form the basis of your company's cultural principles.

Now that you've spent some time reflecting on your personality traits, your preferred working environment, and your core values, you should have a pretty good guide for writing your own list of traits to look for in colleagues. You can ask an AI-based language model for guidance. Here are the suggestions from ChatGPT.

I tend to get along with people when:

- They take initiative and drive projects forward independently.
- They excel in fast-paced, dynamic environments and embrace rapid change.
- They make quick decisions and prefer action over prolonged deliberation.
- They challenge the status quo and are excited by bold, unconventional ideas.
- They value honesty and candor, speaking their mind openly and constructively.

I tend to clash with people when:

- They feel uncomfortable in fast-moving environments and prefer a steady workflow.
- They struggle with making decisions and often overanalyze without acting.
- They prioritize politeness over honesty and shy away from direct communication.
- They favor traditional methods and are uneasy with new, untested ideas.
- They desire detailed plans and guidelines and are uncomfortable with ambiguity or risk.

The lists created by myself and by ChatGPT are quite similar, but I generally prefer the one I came up with myself. Play around with it and see what works best for you.

As your company grows, it's likely that you'll end up hiring some people who aren't the best fit for your personality or working style. These people may go on to be highly valued, successful employees at your company. However, you should place an extreme emphasis on alignment when it comes to your co-founders and any members of your leadership team, because these are the people you'll be working closely with the most. You should also place a strong emphasis on alignment for your first 20 employees, and whenever you end up hiring managers even if they don't report to you directly. This will ensure you have a strong core group of people who you're likely to work well with, and it's these people who will be hiring new talent as you scale up.

Using personality traits as a key factor in hiring decisions bothers some people. If you don't think the tests are reliable, that's fine; come up with your own way to assess personality fit and alignment. In fact, I'm not advocating that you give personality tests to candidates. Instead, I'm advocating that you inform candidates about your personality and values, so that they can make their own decision. I'll also advocate that you use your personality, working environment preferences, and values to create a set of cultural principles for your company, and that you incorporate an assessment of culture fit during the hiring process.

It's a really bad mistake to ignore culture fit entirely. For one thing, if you clash with one of your employees, they also probably clash with you. They will likely be just as unhappy working with you as you will be working with them. It takes two to tango. Why would it be a good idea to subject your future employees to a poor working relationship with their boss? Oh, but management gurus say that you should just adjust your style to accommodate each individual employee. You don't—you absolutely do not have to do that—and you shouldn't. If showing up to work each day at your own company makes you feel like you're walking on eggshells, like you can't be yourself, then you will eventually burn out and quit. Depending on how far along your company is at the time, that could be anywhere from a moderate disruption to a complete catastrophe for your company. So don't listen to that nonsense, you're allowed to have opinions about who you want to work with just like everybody else.

If you hire for skills instead of attitude, then you will eventually lose control of the culture of your company. Culture is determined by behavior. Behavior is determined by person-alities, personal values, and incentives. By the time people become adults, they have learned patterns of behavior that are difficult to change even with strong incentives. In addition, crafting behavior through incentives is a tricky business that often leads to complexity and unintended consequences; just look at the US tax code. If you want people at your company to exhibit certain behaviors and avoid other behaviors—that is, if you want your company to have a certain type of culture—then the most reliable way to get there is to hire people who already behave that way naturally. Nevertheless, it's still helpful to express these concepts as cultural principles so that you can more easily communicate them to potential employees and come up with actions to further incentivise them.

Now that you better understand your own personality traits, your preferred working environment, your personal values, and the traits and anti-traits you'll use as a guide for choosing your future colleagues, you can translate these into some cultural principles for your company. Come up with five cultural principles that describe the culture you want at your company. These cultural principles should be bold, memo-rable, and actionable. To be clear, do not come up with corpo-rate values; instead, come up with actionable principles. These should be things people do, not things people believe. Don't try to bring any nuance into your cultural principles, take a strong stance. If your cultural principles would work for everyone, then you stand for nothing. Your cultural principles should make some people excited, but not everybody; they should turn some people off.

Coming up with a strong set of cultural principles takes some effort. I have found it helpful to use an AI-based language model as a sounding board to generate ideas based on the descriptions I previously wrote for my personality profile, preferred working environment, and personal values. However, it generally takes quite a bit of iteration.

Here are some cultural principles that work for me:

Cultural Principles

Invent or Die

We exist to obliterate conventions, destroy outdated practices, and set new standards. Innovation is our lifeblood, not a department or trend. Creativity and intuition propel us beyond known limits into uncharted territories, where we don't just follow rules—we make them. If it exists, we will reimagine it, improve it, or replace it entirely. Bold risks and unconventional ideas drive us forward because if we're not rewriting the script, we're failing.

Take Immediate Action

We operate with relentless urgency. Bureaucracy, pointless meetings, and hesitation are enemies of progress—we cut through them all to maintain pure focus on immediate results. Action isn't just a preference; it's a mandate. We make bold, instinctive decisions, moving directly from idea to execution. If it doesn't drive us forward now, it doesn't belong. We don't wait for permission; we move, decide, and build now.

Embrace the Battle

We operate with absolute honesty and authenticity. Bullshit and hidden agendas have no place here. Trust is forged through brutal transparency and unwavering integrity.. This is a battleground for the bold. We demand unfiltered honesty and thrive on direct, intense debate. Here, friction is fuel, and only the strongest ideas emerge. Ego is left at the door—there's no room for it when victory demands clear minds and tough skins. We confront challenges head-on, knowing that only through relentless, candid dialogue can we push our ideas to their highest potential. If you can't keep up, don't step up.

Distill to the Core

Complexity is for the unfocused. We cut through the noise, distilling ideas and designs down to their purest, most essential form. Simplicity isn't just beautiful—it's a weapon, a functional imperative that drives relentless impact. Anything unnecessary is discarded; clarity and intuition rule. Genius lies in making the complex feel inevitable, so that every idea, every product, feels as though it could never have been any other way.

Never Relent

We don't chase competitors; we pursue impact. Obstacles are merely fuel, and setbacks only drive us to push harder. We're an unstoppable force, moving relentlessly forward with resilience, grit, and an unbreakable commitment to bend the curve of humanity. When we encounter an obstacle, we say, "Fuck it. We've got this shit." Reaching the summit is just the beginning—once we're there, we're already looking to the horizon for the next mountain to climb.

These cultural principles describe a fast-paced, results-oriented, ambitious, creative, and high-pressure environment. An environment in which we relentlessly pursue a big vision, and push each other to excel through productive conflict rather than harmony. We make decisions quickly, and shift priorities rapidly as we get new information. This would probably not be a great culture for everyone. But, it's a culture that perfectly matches my personality and values. It's the type of work environment that makes me happy and allows me to be successful. It's also optimized to leverage the startup's super-power—speed and agility. And, if I'm starting my own company I can make sure to implement it. Because setting up your company's culture so that it works for you is the most important thing you can do as a founder.

6. Are you able to lead?

I've never met Elon Musk. So, what I'm about to say is based on public perception or, perhaps more accurately, my perception of public perception of Mr. Musk and his leadership style. By and large, people think that Elon is a jerk. Whether he is or isn't actually a jerk is not relevant, what is relevant is that many people still want to go work for his various companies even though he is widely regarded as a jerk. That's interesting! How come? This is the Elon Musk paradox.

Elon is not the first person to illustrate this paradox in leadership. People thought that Steve Jobs was a jerk, but lots of people wanted to go work with him at Apple. Someone actually made a movie about Anna Wintour likening her to the devil! But, lots of people still want to work at Vogue magazine. The phenomenon exists outside of the business world too. General George S. Patton Jr. was often portrayed as an arrogant jerk by the press during World War II—he was even officially reprimanded during the war for *physically slapping* one of his soldiers for trying to get out of his duty—yet no military leader was as respected by their troops as Gen. Patton. [1]

Some people take the wrong lesson from these examples. They think that these examples suggest that being a jerk is a prerequisite to being a good leader. I'm sure there are lots of people who aren't regarded as jerks who are regarded as good leaders, but the media doesn't report on them as much because it's not a juicy story. I do think it's possible that being too nice makes someone a bad leader. On leadership, Patton said, "When you are a leader you are not in a contest to see how happy you can keep the troops. You are not running for public office. You must pick men who can get the job done." [2] In any case, these leaders must have some other characteristics that make people want to go work with them even if they may be difficult to work with. What are these characteristics?

I believe that the vast majority of good leaders possess the following five traits. They are visionary, passionate, decisive, hands on, and set the bar high. While I would also like to believe that leaders should have high integrity, I'm not sure if the data support the idea that it's a necessary trait. Still, integrity would be good too.

Visionary

Nobody wants to bust their ass working on something small. All great leaders choose to go after a compelling mission. Something bigger than themselves or their company. Elon's companies are pushing the boundaries of technological

---

1. General Patton's Principles for Life & Leadership by Porter B. Williamson
2. General Patton's Principles for Life & Leadership by Porter B. Williamson

progress; solving artificial intelligence, building reusable rockets for a mission to Mars, transitioning the world to renewable energy, etc. Apple isn't just building computers, they are building the best products to enrich people's lives so that those who are crazy enough to try to change the world, can. A leader who cannot articulate a compelling vision is a leader of mercenaries.

Passionate

To state the obvious, if you don't actually believe in your vision, then your people will see right through your bullshit. I guarantee it. But it's not enough to believe. You set the ceiling for how enthusiastic anyone else will be about it. If you aren't able to express enthusiasm and passion about your vision to others, then they won't be passionate about it either. Elon isn't the most polished speaker, but watch the section from 60 minutes in which they ask him about his disappointment that Neil Armstrong and other heroes of his from the early space program were coming out against SpaceX and commercial space flight. As he fights back tears, you can see in his eyes how much he cares about the mission. You can't fake caring.

Decisive

Whoever makes the tough decisions is the person in charge. If you are not the person who is making the tough decisions, then you are not the person in charge, regardless of what your title is. Appearing on the Late Show, Anna Wintour said, "I'm very decisive. And, I try to give very clear directions to the people that I'm working with and sometimes, unfortunately, they don't hear the answer that they would like to hear." If you cannot make quick, bold decisions—even when they are unpopular, or when they are shrouded by uncertainty that cannot be eliminated—then you have no business being in a leadership role.

Hands-on

You cannot earn the respect of your employees if you're not able to drill down into the weeds and get hands-on with them when necessary. Particularly in a crisis. Two of General Patton's basic principles of leadership were to "Get up front! Trying to lead from behind makes you a driver, not a leader." and "You must always do everything you ask of the men you command." Do fictional heroes like Gandalf or Aragorn in the Lord of the Rings sit back and watch as their troops head into battle against evil, commanding from afar? Hell no. They are often the first to draw their swords and meet the enemy. That's why they're heroes.

Set the bar high

Everybody who worked with Steve Jobs knew that he wasn't going to accept anything unless it was insanely great. He drove people to achieve more than they ever thought they could. People wanted to work with Steve, in part, because they knew he would make them better. An interviewer once asked Steve, "What does it mean when you tell someone their work is shit?," and he responded, "Uh, it usually means their work is shit. Sometimes it means, 'I think your work is shit, and I'm wrong.' But usually it means their work is not anywhere near good enough. When you've got really good people, they know they're really good, and you don't have to baby people's egos so much. And what really matters is the work. And everybody knows that: That's all that matters—is the work. . . . And the most important thing, I think, you can do for somebody who's really good and who's really being counted on is to point out to them when their work isn't good enough." You don't need to be as rude as Steve was, but you do need to set a high bar for yourself and everyone around you.

If you can exhibit these leadership traits—if you are visionary, passionate, decisive, hands-on, and set a high bar—while still coming across as jolly and nice, then more power to you. But, it's more important to lead effectively than to be liked.

Earlier, I said that I'm not aware of any convincing research linking founder's personality traits to the success of their startups. That's true. I also said that I don't think someone's personality traits are good or bad, they just are. That's also true. But, at the same time, I don't think that someone can be an effective leader if they can't articulate a big vision, if they don't exude passion for that vision, if they can't be decisive when it counts, get hands-on when it's needed, or set a high bar for themselves and their employees. Some of these leadership characteristics are probably correlated with personality traits, and you should be really honest with yourself about whether or not you have them before deciding if you should be the CEO of your company. Not everyone has what it takes.

Part Two
Hiring Others

7. Typical roles in a startup.

I've never met anybody great who cares a lot about their job title. Job titles are what mediocre people care about. Responsibilities and impact are what great people care about. That said, even though job titles are largely irrelevant for early stage startups, roles are extremely important. Before you hire anybody, you should list out the roles that your startup needs to fill. Roles don't equate to people, however. Each person will likely have to take on multiple roles in the beginning. However, it's important that each person knows which roles they are responsible for, and it's important for you to know that all of the roles your company needs are covered. The following is a non-exhaustive list of some roles you should consider for your startup.

Here are concise descriptions for each role:

Vision: Define and communicate the long-term direction and purpose of the company to both internal and external audiences.

Strategy: Develop and communicate a set of strategic principles to guide decision-making at your company.

Culture: Shape and maintain the company's values, behaviors, and working environment to foster a productive team.

Fundraising: Secure financial resources by pitching to investors, managing relationships, and overseeing funding rounds.

Board Management: Facilitate communication with the board of directors, preparing reports, and managing expectations.

Product Management: Define product goals, prioritize features, and ensure that the product meets customer and market needs.

Product Design: Design the product's functionality, appearance, and user experience to meet customer needs and business goals.

Product Marketing: Create messaging and positioning that communicate the product's value to customers, supporting sales efforts.

Research and Development: Innovate and develop new technologies, products, or features to keep the company ahead of potential competitors.

Software Engineering: Build, test, and maintain software applications that form the core of the product or service.

Hardware Engineering: Design and develop physical products or components, ensuring they meet performance and cost criteria.

DevOps: Ensure smooth deployment, monitoring, and scaling of applications by managing infrastructure and development pipelines.

Information Technology: Manage internal systems, tools, and technologies that support day-to-day operations and workflows.

Information Security: Protect the company's digital assets and data by implementing security policies and responding to threats.

Sales: Drive revenue by identifying leads, converting prospects, and managing customer relationships.

Sales Operations: Optimize sales processes, tools, and metrics to enhance sales performance and efficiency.

Customer Support: Resolve customer issues and provide assistance to ensure a positive experience and retention.

Market Research: Gather and analyze market data to inform product development, marketing strategies, and business decisions.

Marketing: Develop campaigns and strategies to attract customers, build awareness, and grow the brand.

Branding: Craft the company's identity, including its visual style, tone, and public image.

Communications: Manage internal and external messaging to ensure clear and consistent information flow across stakeholders.

Public Relations: Build and maintain the company's reputation by engaging with the media and managing public-facing messages.

Operations: Manage the daily logistics, resources, and processes that keep the company running smoothly.

Supply Chain: Manage the sourcing of materials, production, inventory, and distribution of physical products to ensure they are delivered to customers efficiently and cost-effectively.

Financial Planning: Forecast financial performance, manage budgets, and ensure the company stays on track to meet its financial goals.

Accounting: Track financial transactions, ensure accurate reporting, and maintain compliance with tax and financial regulations.

Human Resources: Manage hiring, performance, and employee well-being to build a strong and motivated team.

Legal: Handle contracts, intellectual property, and legal risks to protect the company's interests.

Regulatory: Ensure compliance with industry regulations, standards, and government laws applicable to the company.

Again, these are just some examples of roles that are commonly required at many different types of startups. They are not job titles. In the beginning, each person will likely cover multiple roles. And, as you grow, you'll eventually have multiple people in each role. I've tried to order the roles so that similar roles are grouped together in the list. Your startup will likely require some of these roles, and it may require some roles that are not on the list. You should adapt this list to your needs by creating a list of the roles you think you'll need at your startup. I also recommend ordering the roles by how important you think they are right now, and by how well you and your co-founders can cover them. You should focus on hiring people for roles that are important, but aren't covered well by the current team.

8. Let the right ones in.

There's an old saying that your company culture is determined by who you hire, fire, and promote. It's 100% true. If you hire the right kinds of people, then your company will develop the culture you want. If you don't hire the right types of people, then you'll wake up one day at a company you no longer recognize asking yourself, "Well, how did I get here?". It doesn't matter how often you repeat your values or cultural principles or even if you write them on the wall of your office, for the most part the people you hire are going to continue to behave the same way they did before you hired them. Therefore, if you want people at your company to behave in certain ways—such as being decisive, or offering solutions instead of complaints—then you simply need to hire people who already do those things naturally. Approximately 80% of management is just hiring people who are a great fit for your company, and firing people who aren't a great fit for your company. The concept is simple, but the execution is difficult.

Step one, which you completed in part one, is defining your company's cultural principles and the personality traits of people you are compatible with, and writing those down in a personal user guide that you will give to any potential co-founders or candidates before you decide to work together. If you've done this well—by writing a set of clear and controversial cultural principles—then some people will simply drop out of the process at that point. But, so many companies have professed cultural principles they don't actually follow that many people will discount whatever you send them; to be honest, many may not even read it. They will assume that your cultural principles are empty words just like everyone else's. That, surely you don't mean them. Adding a small amount of structure to your hiring process can help make sure you hire people who will fit the culture you're trying to create more often than not, and will give you the tools to fix problems when you do make hiring mistakes.

Before we move on to talk about the process of hiring employees, it's important to cover the topic of finding good co-founders for your startup. Even though people get together to start companies with the best of intentions, co-founder breakup is a common cause of startup failures. Therefore, it's incredibly important to find co-founders who are aligned with your big vision, complement your skill sets with their own areas of comparative advantage, have compatible personality traits, share the same values, and fit with your natural leadership style and the cultural principles of the company you want to build. It's difficult to find co-founders who will check each of those boxes, but you shouldn't compromise. So, ideally you've written your personal user guide already and can use that to start the conversation with potential co-founders. But, if you've already started your company and you already have co-founders, and are just now reading this book, then I suggest you take a three day retreat together to get alignment on all of these things. These conversations will probably be difficult, but it's better to have them upfront than when your company has 100 or more employees depending on you.

Once you've identified a group of co-founders who are aligned with your big vision, complement your skill sets with their own areas of comparative advantage, have compatible personality traits, share your same values, and fit with your natural leadership style and the cultural principles of the company you want to build, then it's time to actually form your company. Most of the details on how to structure your company will be taken care of by your legal counsel, and I suggest you try to retain the best corporate counsel you can find because it will help down the road. Aside from that, I have a few unconventional suggestions on how to set up a company with multiple co-founders so that it has the best chance for long-term success.

As Founder and CEO of a company, you are ultimately responsible for all aspects of that company's performance. You set the vision and define the cultural principles. Every other person at the company reports to you, and you have the ultimate say in who to hire and who to fire. You will be the primary point of contact for investors, and have to be the face of the company during the fundraising process. If you're selling to other businesses, then you will probably have a major role in the sales process for many years, even if you don't want to. If there's a problem that nobody else can figure out how to solve, it will find its way to your desk. When things go well, you will be expected to give credit to the team. And, when things don't go well, you will be expected to take the blame. If the company fails on your watch, it's your fault and it's your reputation that will suffer. If you haven't done it before, then I can tell you the job is much more stressful and difficult than you can imagine. Even people who have spent a long career in the C-suite are often overwhelmed when they finally step into the CEO role. In my own case, I remember spending the night in a San Francisco emergency room worried I was having a heart attack; thankfully, it was only a panic attack due to my frayed emotional state and deteriorating mental health. Nobody who is doing the CEO job well thinks it's fun. So, if you really want to take on the job, you should be compensated for it.

In addition to the fact that the Founder and CEO will take on more stress and responsibility than the other co-founders, they also need to be able to drive the company in the direction they see fit. The absolute worst situation to be in is one in which you have responsibility for delivering results and are accountable for those results, but don't have the agency to pursue them in the way you think is best. I believe the Founder and CEO should look at data, take other's opinions into account, and solicit feedback while they are making the decision about which path to take towards the summit, but once they make that decision it is their way or the highway. And, that's true for everyone else at the company from individual contributors, to leadership, to co-founders. It's even mostly true of the board in my view, but I'll cover that in a later chapter. To ensure that the Founder and CEO has this agency, I believe the company should be set up to give them voting power.

A lot of advice suggests that founders should split equity equally, or as equally as possible. My advice is to split equity as equally as possible, except that the person who will be taking on the CEO role should receive 51% of the initial shares of the company to give them voting power. To be more precise, I'm assuming that the company is being formed before taking any external investment. Ownership percentages will obviously change once the company raises capital by selling shares.

I don't think the number of co-founders you have matters very much, as long as you choose them wisely and set your company up properly. If there are two co-founders, then split the equity 51% to the CEO and 49% to the other co-founder. If there are three co-founders, then split the equity 51% to the CEO and 24.5% to each of the other co-founders. The more co-founders you have, the more unequal the initial distribution of equity and the more difficult this conversation will be. If this is too difficult of a conversation to have, or you can't get agreement with your co-founders, then you shouldn't be starting a company together anyway. Countries need checks and balances on power because it's difficult to emigrate to another country, but startups need a single person in charge because it helps them move quickly, and if someone doesn't like how that person is running the company they can find a job someplace else relatively easily. Startups don't need checks and balances, at least not at the early stages.

Finally, after you get agreement on the equity structure, you should try to write out roles and responsibilities for each of the co-founders as clearly as possible. At the same time, keep these flexible. I do not believe that formal job titles are necessary, useful, or even a good idea at this stage of a company. Even if the Founder and CEO takes on a particularly challenging role, all of the founders are taking on an unusually risky endeavor. The entire founding team is special. They'll likely be the ones stepping up to the plate at the most important moments throughout the life of your company. You don't want them pigeonholed in some particular role, you want them all rolling up their sleeves and pitching in on whatever is necessary. Therefore, I think founding stage startups should just give people titles like "Founder (Engineering)" or "Founder (Sales)". You don't need to worry about giving people "real job titles" until you are recruiting more senior roles, which you should probably delay until you have at least 25 people.

There is an old saying that startups should be slow to hire, and quick to fire. In part, this is important because you don't want to run out of money. Many startups make a mistake by growing headcount too quickly, and their expenses get out of control. But, a bigger reason why this is sage advice is that the most important characteristic of a good employee for your startup is that they fit well according to your cultural principles; that they have the right attitude you're looking for. Culture fit is impossible to assess from a resume, and difficult to assess in general. Skills are relatively easy to assess, at least for technical roles, but a person's attitude will determine how successful they become at your startup. In fact, it's especially important to avoid hiring people with the wrong attitude. A single person with the wrong attitude can create negative value for your company, and add a cultural debt that takes a long time to repay.

It took me a long time to come up with a process that properly accounts for culture fit in hiring decisions. The process is quite simple and easy to implement, which is good because I am generally not a fan of processes. A culture fit assessment should be a part of the interview process for every candidate. It should consist of three questions, graded on a scale from 1 to 5, designed to assess the character and personality traits you're looking for in future colleagues. Make sure that your culture fit assessment includes a clear grading rubric. An AI-based language model can help you draft this assessment from the user guide you wrote in part one. A score of less than 3 out of 5 on any question disqualifies a candidate, as does an overall score of less than 12.

No matter what the other circumstances are, the outcome of the culture fit assessment cannot be overturned by anyone, including you. Ideally, the culture fit assessment should be given early in the interview process, such as after a review of the candidate's resume and an initial phone screen. Someone other than the hiring manager should be tasked with giving the culture fit assessment because the hiring manager will always feel pressure to fill the role, which could cause them to subconsciously inflate candidates' scores. In addition, the culture interviewer should be blinded to the candidate's background. They should not receive the candidate's resume or look them up on LinkedIn nor should they receive feedback from other interviewers; in fact, they should preferably only get the candidate's first name. This way the cultural assessment is essentially blinded. I have found myself to be easily swayed by certain experiences, like going to the same college as I did (the University of Michigan) or previous experience working at a well-known company, to the extent that even I overlook problems of culture fit. This process was designed to prevent these biases from influencing the hiring process.

Here's an example of a cultural assessment I created for my hypothetical company based on the cultural principles described earlier:

Culture Fit Assessment for a 20-Minute Interview

<u>Instructions for Interviewer:</u>

This concise interview is designed to assess the candidate's alignment with our company's cultural principles. Please ask the following three questions, scoring each from 1 to 5 using the provided rubric. A score below 3 on any question or a total score below 12 out of 15 will result in the candidate's elimination from the selection process.

Important Notes:

- Focus solely on the candidate's cultural fit.
- Encourage specific examples from past experiences.
- Assess innovation, urgency, resilience, simplicity, authenticity, and direct communication.
- Use the rubrics consistently for objective scoring.

Time Management:

- Introduction: 2 minutes
- Each Question: 5 minutes (total of 15 minutes)
- Candidate's response: ~3 minutes
- Follow-up questions: ~2 minutes
- Closing: 3 minutes

Question 1: Innovation and Simplification

"Can you share an example of when you innovated or reinvented something in a way that simplified a complex problem to its core essence? How did you challenge existing norms, and what was the impact?"

Attributes Assessed:

- Inventiveness and Creativity
- Ability to Distill Complexity into Simplicity
- Challenging Conventions

Rubric for Scoring Question 1:

- 5 (Excellent):
    - Provided a specific example of innovative thinking that simplified a complex issue.
    - Challenged existing norms significantly.
    - Resulted in substantial positive impact.
- 4 (Good):
    - Shared a clear instance of innovation and simplification.
    - Positively impacted the project or organization.
- 3 (Average):

- Offered an example with some innovation or simplification.
    - Impact was moderate.
- 2 (Below Average):
    - Example lacked originality or effective simplification.
    - Minimal impact.
- 1 (Poor):
    - Unable to provide an example.
    - Resistant to innovation or simplification.

Question 2: Urgency, Resilience, and Relentless Pursuit

"Describe a situation where you had to take immediate action in the face of significant obstacles or setbacks. How did you handle the challenges, and what were the results?"

Attributes Assessed:

- Sense of Urgency
- Resilience and Grit
- Relentless Focus on Results

Rubric for Scoring Question 2:

- 5 (Excellent):
    - Detailed a high-pressure situation requiring swift action.
    - Demonstrated exceptional resilience and grit.
    - Overcame obstacles, leading to significant success.
- 4 (Good):

- ○ Provided an example of acting promptly and persistently.
  - ○ Achieved positive outcomes despite challenges.
- 3 (Average):
  - ○ Example included timely action with some perseverance.
  - ○ Outcome was satisfactory.
- 2 (Below Average):
  - ○ Showed hesitation or struggled with challenges.
  - ○ Limited success.
- 1 (Poor):
  - ○ Avoided action or gave up when faced with obstacles.
  - ○ Negative results.

Question 3: Authenticity and Embracing Conflict

"Tell me about a time when you engaged in a direct, intense debate or had to be brutally honest to push an idea forward. How did you approach the situation, and what was the outcome?"

Attributes Assessed:

- Brutal Transparency and Honesty
- Willingness to Engage in Direct, Intense Debate
- Collaboration Through Conflict

Rubric for Scoring Question 3:

- 5 (Excellent):

- o Provided a specific instance of direct, honest communication in a challenging context.
- o Demonstrated the ability to handle conflict constructively.
- o Led to stronger ideas or solutions.
- 4 (Good):
  - o Shared an example of honest dialogue or debate.
  - o Resulted in positive outcomes.
- 3 (Average):
  - o Example involved some honest communication.
  - o Outcome was acceptable.
- 2 (Below Average):
  - o Hesitant to be direct or engage in conflict.
  - o Limited effectiveness.
- 1 (Poor):
  - o Avoided honesty or mishandled conflict.
  - o Negative consequences ensued.

Final Steps:

- Total the scores from all three questions (maximum of 15).
- Assess the results:
  - o Eliminate any candidate scoring less than 3 on any question.
  - o Eliminate any candidate with a total score below 10.
  - o Provide brief notes citing specific elements from the candidate's responses to justify your scores.

Additional Interviewer Tips:

- Be Mindful of Time: Keep the conversation focused within the allotted time.
- Encourage Specificity: Guide candidates to provide detailed, relevant examples.
- Active Listening: Pay attention to assess multiple attributes.
- Effective Probing: Use follow-up questions to elicit necessary details.
- Maintain Objectivity: Use the rubrics for consistent scoring.

After a candidate has passed the cultural assessment, then it's time to assess their skills. I believe that the best way to do this is to have them prepare and give a presentation on a topic of your choice. For example, you could have a software engineer give a presentation about continuous integration. You could have an AI researcher give a presentation on alternatives to softmax attention. You could have a sales representative give a mock sales pitch for a chosen product or service. Obviously, choose the topic of the presentation so that it's relevant for their role. Ask them to prepare a 30 minute presentation, but schedule the meeting for 1.5 hours. Invite a few other relevant people from your company to the presentation, and pepper the candidate with questions for the whole 1.5 hours. You'll figure out if they know their stuff, if they can communicate effectively, and test their ability to perform under pressure. After the presentation, take the candidate out for lunch or dinner to see how you all get along in a (relatively) social setting.

Lastly, check the candidate's references personally before you provide them with a written offer. I can't stress this step enough, checking a candidate's references is not optional; it's by far the most important part of the interview process. For example, Jensen Huang says ""My method is always I go back to reference checks and I ask them the questions that I was going to ask the candidate. And the reason for that is you could always make for a great moment, but it's hard for you to run away from your past."[1] In order to check references, ask the candidate to provide you with three references, preferably their direct managers or direct reports from previous jobs. If you're hiring someone straight out of school, this could also include the candidate's professors or academic advisors. Schedule 30-45 minute calls with at least 2 of the provided references. Ask the references to rate the candidate on a scale from 1 to 10, where 1 is the worst person they ever worked with in that role and 10 is the best person they ever worked with in that role. If the reference rates the candidate as a 9 or 10, ask them to think of a person they worked with who was a 7 or 8 and describe what specific attributes set the candidate apart. On the other hand, if the reference rates the candidate a 7 or 8, ask them to think of a person they worked with who as a 9 or 10 and describe in what specific areas the candidate would need to improve on to get to that level. In both cases, ask them to give you specific examples. Next, go through your cultural assessment with the reference asking them to answer the questions on behalf of the candidate.

At the end of this process, you'll have a good sense if this

---

1. https://www.entrepreneur.com/business-news/how-nvidia-ceo-jensen-huang-interviews-hires-new-employees/481122

candidate is a good fit for your company and the role, or not. You—the Founder and CEO—make the final call on whether to make an offer to the candidate. Even if they will be reporting to someone else, even if everyone else thought they were the best thing since sliced bread, it's your decision. Make sure everyone involved in the process commits to that upfront too. If you believe the candidate is a good fit for the role, you have to switch into selling mode. Get them into the seat. Use market data to guide your initial offer—you can find this online or through service providers like Carta—but you should be willing to negotiate if they got a great cultural assessment, did well in their onsite presentation, and had great references. And sell them on your vision, make them believe they'll change the world by working with you, that's one of the key reasons for crafting a big, exciting vision in the first place. When you send the written offer, include a copy of your user guide with it and ask them to read it before deciding to join the team. Also, make sure that the offer letter includes a provision stating that you'll conduct a review of their performance after 3 months on the job; I'll discuss this in more detail in the next chapter.

If this process sounds like it could make hiring difficult, because most candidates will fail, you're correct. Most candidates will fail. That is a feature, not a bug. A good rule of thumb based on my past experience is that roughly 50 to 75% of applicants will be ruled out by the culture fit assessment! Especially for your first 50 hires or so, you need to try your best to make sure they are great candidates who are aligned with your vision and cultural principles. You'll still make some hiring mistakes, but this process will keep them to a minimum.

If a candidate or new hire asks a lot of questions about career development prospects at your startup, that's a bad sign. Getting promoted at a startup requires three things. First, and most importantly, your startup must need to fill a more senior role. This is a crucial point, you should never succumb to the idea that people should get promoted because they deserve it, because they've been with you a certain amount of time, or even because they've got offers to move to other companies. Your job as the Founder and CEO is to do what's best for your company, not to improve your employees' resumes. After all, the number one thing that will improve their resume is having worked at a startup that is winning; so make winning your number one priority. Second, the employee should be an exemplar of your cultural principles as judged by you and through 360 feedback; they should not just be an alright cultural fit, they should be exceptional. Third, the employee should have delivered key results for your company. If you determine that you have a need for a more senior role and you have an employee who could fill that role who is a great culture fit and who has demonstrated they can deliver key results for your company, then it's a no brainer—promote them. You should write out a policy that says this clearly and make sure every new hire gets it and reads it on day one.

I have pretty strong feelings about what it takes for someone to succeed at a startup. To be frank, working at a startup is not for everyone. In fact, it's not for most people. The people who make great startup employees are exceptional. They have an unusual combination of high agency and high risk tolerance. A person with high agency is someone who exhibits a strong sense of control over their actions, choices, and impact on their environment. They believe in their ability to shape their circumstances and are proactive in seeking solutions rather than waiting for external influences to dictate outcomes. High-agency individuals tend to:

- Take initiative and actively pursue goals and rarely need external prompting.
- Solve problems because they see obstacles as challenges to overcome rather than reasons to quit.
- Assume responsibility and take ownership of their successes and failures, seeing both as opportunities for growth.
- Have confidence in their abilities and in their capacity to make meaningful decisions and effect change.
- Exhibit resilience and back quickly from setbacks, using adversity as fuel to push forward.
- Drive results and are oriented toward action and tangible outcomes, usually seeking measurable success over theoretical plans.

High agency is especially valuable in startup cultures where resilience, independence, and a results-driven approach are essential. In fact, the traits that make someone a good startup employee may actually make them a bad fit for a career at a large, legacy corporation. The following list summarizes my opinions on what makes someone a great fit for startup life.

Good Startup Employee vs Bad Startup Employee

Good Startup Employee

- Challenges existing norms and questions assumptions to drive innovation.
- Acts with urgency, focusing on rapid progress toward goals.
- Takes ownership of decisions and is accountable for outcomes.
- Sets clear, ambitious goals with specific timelines.
- Communicates clearly and directly, offering solutions rather than complaints.
- Embraces conflict as a means to improve ideas and products.
- Builds empathy with customers to anticipate their needs.
- Designs simple, user-friendly solutions to complex problems.
- Rapidly iterates, learning quickly from experiments and feedback.
- Aligns actions with the company's mission and long-term vision.
- Holds self and teammates accountable, fostering mutual responsibility.
- Is authentic, honest, and transparent in all interactions.
- Thinks creatively, pushing the boundaries of what's possible.
- Is mentally tough, handling challenges with resilience.

- Balances bold action with pragmatic consideration of results.
- Recognizes when a solution meets high standards and avoids wasting time on unnecessary polish.
- Proactively seeks feedback and over-communicates to ensure alignment.
- Takes calculated risks, understanding the potential impacts.
- Maintains focus amidst external challenges, avoiding unnecessary pivots.
- Prioritizes collective success over individual interests.
- Is able to pivot with purpose but also to stick to a course when necessary.

Bad Startup Employee

- Accepts the status quo without question, hindering innovation.
- Defaults to safe choices, missing transformative opportunities.
- Prioritizes processes and tools over achieving meaningful results.
- Avoids taking responsibility, deflecting decisions and outcomes.
- Seeks consensus to evade individual accountability.
- Communicates indirectly or withholds information, causing confusion.
- Complains without offering solutions, contributing to a negative environment.
- Invests excessive time in planning to avoid taking action.

- Is afraid to fail, leading to stagnation and missed opportunities.
- Over-engineers solutions, adding unnecessary complexity.
- Focuses on short-term tasks without considering the bigger picture.
- Engages in dishonest or insincere behavior, eroding trust.
- Is overly cautious, avoiding risks that could lead to significant gains.
- Is sensitive or passive-aggressive, impeding open communication.
- Fails to seek or provide timely feedback, resulting in misalignment.
- Pivots frequently without strategic rationale, losing direction.
- Strives for perfection, causing delays and hindering progress.
- Does not hold self or others accountable for commitments.
- Prioritizes personal agendas over the company's mission.
- Relies heavily on theory without applying practical action.
- Avoids conflict, missing opportunities to improve through constructive debate.

9. Move the wrong ones out.

Many founders in the technology industry start their companies relatively early in their careers, before the corporate world has had the chance to beat them into submission. This gives them the benefit of optimism, and the audacity to believe they can start a company and change the world. These are amazing advantages. Nevertheless, there are many things that are best learned through experience.

At the time I started my first company, I had never fired anyone. I had been an individual contributor in all of my previous roles. To be honest, I did not expect it to be very difficult for me, given my naturally low agreeableness. In fact, while I found out that the act of firing someone was not particularly difficult, making the decision to fire someone was very difficult. Even though my personality profile may suggest otherwise, I was initially quite hesitant to get rid of people, and gave people many chances to turn around poor performance or a clear lack of culture fit (which I now know simply can't be turned around). Sometimes, I even diverted responsibility for the decision away from myself and onto the hiring manager; a terrible lapse in leadership.

Through many years of experience, I learned the following lessons about firing people that I hope to pass along; though, I will repeat that these principles are difficult to learn without making some mistakes and getting the scar tissue yourself—so don't beat yourself up too badly if you make some mistakes in the beginning.

First, if you are the founder and CEO then it is absolutely your responsibility—and within your authority—to make the decision to terminate someone's employment at your company even if that person doesn't report to you directly. That is part of sitting in the big chair. To be clear, you should also expect your managers to make these difficult decisions too, and you should hold them accountable for doing that, but if you believe that someone in your company is underperforming or is a poor culture fit then you should move them along yourself.

Second, if you're reading this book then you are building an ambitious startup with an important mission, and you'll be trying to hire the best and brightest people to help you achieve your vision. Even if these people are all extremely talented, many of them will simply be a bad match for the company you're trying to build. However, they are probably a great match for another company with a different vision and culture. Letting them go enables them to find a company or role that works better for them. If you're hiring great people in the first place, you don't usually need to worry about what will happen to them if you let them go—they'll land on their feet with a new job soon enough.

Third, if left to your own devices (i.e., without a process), you will almost certainly make the decision to fire someone too slowly. That's human nature. Especially for a first time founder. Even I—with a 6 out of 100 agreeableness score—was way too slow to fire people. At a startup, you don't have the luxury of waiting for people to figure out how to perform at a high level. You need great people now, not tomorrow. Joining a startup is like jumping into the deep end of the pool, and your employees should know they'll be expected to hit the ground running. And, if someone is not performing at a high level, then they can't keep working at your company. It feels harsh, many of us want to give people lots of time to learn the ropes, but your company simply can't afford it while it remains in the startup phase.

And, fourth, negative value add is real. There is a meme in the technology industry that a few people are 10x engineers, most people 1x engineers, and some others are just 0.5x engineers. That is, there are a handful of great engineers who are just way better than average. But, this misses a key piece of information; there are also -10x engineers! Note that this is true for all types of roles, I'm just using engineering as an example because of the pre-existing meme. In fact, negative value employees are much more common than 10x employees! A negative value employee slows down the work—decreases the productivity—of everyone around them. This almost always happens when (i) someone at your company does not buy into your vision or (ii) they are a poor fit according to your cultural principles. It's especially bad if this person is a manager, in which case they can tank the productivity of entire organizations within your company. This person may be extremely talented, they may be friendly and people may like them personally, but they need to go right away. You cannot wait.

Some of my initial hesitation to get rid of people could have been prevented, I think, if I had known what is typical for a startup. According to well-known internet entrepreneur and investor Marc Andreesen, "If you are super-scrupulous about your hiring process, you'll still have maybe a 70% success rate of a new person really working out—if you're lucky. And that's for individual contributors. If you're hiring executives, you'll probably only have a 50% success rate. That's life." [1] That is, you should expect to turn over 3 out of every 10 individual contributors you hire. And, you should expect to turn over 1 out of every 2 executives you hire (once you get your company to the Vice President stage). That's a lot! That's way higher than I realized, and significantly higher than typical turnover rates at large, legacy organizations. Working at a startup is difficult, as I've said a number of times in this book, and it's not for everybody.

Unfortunately, you need to accept the fact that if you want to be founder and CEO, then you're going to have to fire people; pretty frequently too. If you don't think you can get comfortable with that, then I don't think you should start a company.

There is one other decision that is even more difficult than firing someone, and that is when you have to terminate an employee (usually multiple employees) through no fault of

---

1. https://pmarchive.com/how_to_hire_the_best_people.html

their own. This could happen because you've had a financial setback and need to cut costs in order to survive. It could also happen because your company has changed priorities, or pivoted, and those roles no longer fit with your new direction. I faced this latter scenario and struggled with it. I tried, repeatedly, to convince people that they needed to radically change what they were doing so that we could make a quick change in direction. Unfortunately, I learned a difficult lesson. It's easier to change your people, than to get your people to change. You'll probably have to make a decision like this yourself if your startup survives long enough, and it'll be hard, and you'll probably put it off for too long. Again, it's human nature. But this book aims to tell you what you need to hear, not what you want to hear. The earlier you mentally prepare yourself for this possibility, the better.

Elon Musk famously sent an email to all of the employees at then Twitter approximately one month after taking over the company asking them to commit to creating an extremely hardcore culture characterized by long hours at high intensity, or to resign immediately in exchange for three months severance.[2] Technically, the email included a link employees had to order to opt-in on the new Twitter 2.0. Of course, he received a lot of criticism for this email. And, indeed, I think Elon made a mistake in sending it. He should have sent it on day one.

When General Patton took over command of the I Armored

---

2. https://www.cnbc.com/2022/11/16/elon-musk-demands-twitter-staff-commit-to-long-hours-or-leave.html

Corps a few weeks after the bombing of Pearl Harbor at the beginning of WWII, he started his first meeting with the officers by announcing, "I have orders for the transfer of every officer of the I Armored Corps! Every order is signed and dated today. Every officer refusing to run a mile or wanting a transfer will leave this command before the sun goes down!" He made this announcement 80 years before Elon sent his extremely hardcore memo to Twitter employees.

Quite simply, you cannot have people at your company who are not bought into your vision or the culture that you want. If you are taking over an existing company that is highly profitable, you may be able to implement your desired cultural changes gradually. But, by definition, that company is not a startup! You cannot implement changes gradually at a startup, you must act quickly and decisively. Both Elon and Gen. Patton had the difficult task of taking over an existing organization in a time of great peril to find out that this organization did not have the culture they believed it needed to be successful. The resulting actions had to be extreme. Thankfully, you are not taking over an existing organization. So you don't have to take extreme, and painful, actions like this as long as you remain diligent and create the culture you want every step of the way. Moving one person out who is a bad fit for your company today, prevents you from having to let go of hundreds of people later on.

If a new employee is doing a great job, and is a great fit for your culture, you'll usually figure it out pretty quickly.

Conversely, if someone is doing a really bad job—perhaps they are way underqualified for the role you hired them for—or a terrible culture fit, you'll usually figure it out pretty quickly. By pretty quickly, I mean within 2 months. The more difficult, and more common, scenario will be all the people somewhere in between great and terrible. A helpful policy is to force yourself to make a decision about every employee after their first 3 months on the job.

As a side note, I'm writing this chapter (really, this whole book) from the point of view of someone in the United States. In the US, most states have "at-will" employment laws, which means that either the employer or the employee can terminate the employment at any time and for any reason (as long as the reason is not illegal, such as discrimination against an employee for belonging to a protected class). Therefore, I suggest that you consult with legal counsel if you are employing people outside of the US, or in states that do not have at-will employment. In fact, I suggest you consult with legal counsel regardless.

In essence, I recommend you create a policy at your company that all new hires have a 90 day probationary period. Within their first 90 days, usually towards the end of the period but there's no reason to wait if the decision is already obvious, you (or their manager, once your company is large enough) will conduct a performance review of every new hire. Every single new hire, without exception.[3] In fact, you should incorporate

---

3. Even with co-founders, I suggest scheduling a time 90 days after starting your company to sit down together and make the decision—and commitment —to keep moving forward or not.

some language into your standard employee offer letters that explains your process and if you'll offer any severance to employees terminated after 90 days (again, consult with legal counsel). I recommend that you discuss this policy with candidates during the interview process as well. To conduct the performance review, you'll need to draft a 90-day check in form that assesses their overall performance and how well they model your cultural principles on a 1-to-5 scale similar to the cultural assessment in your interview process. You should also include some space for reviewers to provide free form comments or suggestions, because even great employees will have things they could improve on and you should capture that feedback to help them in their professional development.

Here's an example 90 day check in form I created for my hypothetical company:

90-Day Check-In Assessment for New Hires

Purpose

This assessment evaluates the new hire's alignment with our cultural principles, job performance, and potential at their 90-day check-in. Feedback will inform decisions about their continued employment and development within the company. Input will be collected from 3-4 colleagues who have directly worked with the new hire. Scores will be averaged, and comments summarized to provide a comprehensive evaluation.

Instructions for Colleagues

- Confidentiality: Your individual responses will be confidential and aggregated with feedback from other colleagues.
- Honesty and Objectivity: Provide honest, objective feedback based on your direct interactions with the new hire.
- Specific Examples: Include specific examples to support your ratings and comments.
- Rating Scale: For each question, rate the new hire on a scale from 1 to 5:
  - 1 = Does Not Meet Expectations
  - 2 = Below Expectations
  - 3 = Meets Expectations
  - 4 = Exceeds Expectations
  - 5 = Significantly Exceeds Expectations

Assessment Questions

Question 1: Innovation and Willingness to Challenge Conventions

"How well does the new hire demonstrate innovation, creativity, and a willingness to challenge conventions?"

Rating (1-5):

Comments: Provide examples where the new hire reimagined or reinvented a process, product, or solution in an impactful way.

Question 2: Sense of Urgency and Immediate Action

"To what extent does the new hire demonstrate a relentless sense of urgency and decisiveness in achieving results?"

Rating (1-5):

Comments: Share instances where the new hire took immediate, impactful action, cutting through obstacles to drive results.

Question 3: Authenticity, Direct Communication, and Resilience in Conflict

"How effectively does the new hire demonstrate authenticity, direct communication, and resilience, especially when engaging in challenging conversations or debates?"

Rating (1-5):

Comments: Provide examples where the new hire engaged in direct, honest dialogue or debate to push ideas forward and showed resilience in facing difficult situations.

Question 4: Clarity and Quality of Work

"How would you rate the new hire's ability to distill complex issues to their core and produce high-quality, impactful work?"

Rating (1-5):

Comments: Share examples that reflect the new hire's ability to simplify complexity, maintain clarity in their work, and deliver high standards consistently.

Question 5: Potential to Become World-Class in Their Current Role

"To what extent does the new hire demonstrate the potential to become world-class in their current position?"

Rating (1-5):

Comments: Provide observations indicating the new hire's potential for outstanding achievement and impact in their role.

Final Comments

Additional Feedback: Please share any other observations about the new hire that haven't been covered above. Focus on constructive feedback that can aid their professional development.

You should fill out this form yourself and you should have around 3 other people fill it out too. Compute the average scores for each question, and use a language model like ChatGPT to integrate, summarize, and anonymize any written comments. Then, send this summary report to the recent hire, along with a copy to whoever is in charge of human resources at your startup for documentation purposes, and set up a time to talk with them. If the new hire receives an average below a 3 on any question, then you should terminate their employment after 90 days because it's not working out. The same goes if you—just you—give them below a 3 on any of the culture fit questions. Life is too short to work with people you don't like working with. On the other hand, if the new hire is meeting or exceeding expectations then you should give them this feedback and discuss if there are any things they could do to get even better.

Just because you've determined that someone isn't a good fit for your company doesn't mean that they are a bad person, or that they aren't talented and destined for massive success in another environment. The same goes for when an employee is the one who determines they aren't a good fit for your company and resigns. It's important to keep this in mind and treat people with respect. I'm generally in favor of having a policy for severance that's a bit better than what's normal in your market, but it's your call and it depends on the culture you're trying to incentivize at your company. In some cases, it may be appropriate to provide a letter of recommendation for someone you've let go, or to offer to pay for recruiting services who can help them find a new role. Again, making this decision will probably feel bad, but your ex-employees are talented and will land on their feet.

In my experience, people remaining at your company may ask you to justify your decision to them—do not do that, just tell them the decision is final and that you can't share any details. First, you should respect the privacy of the person you just let go; telling everyone why you let them go is effectively talking behind their back. Second, it's your company, you're the CEO, and it's within your authority to make personnel decisions; you don't have to justify yourself. And, whatever you do, don't behave like one of the leaders at a previous company I worked at and tell your employees "I fired those people because they were bad at their jobs, and if you all don't start working harder I'm going to fire you too!"

10. Leave the chair empty.

The biggest mistake that any manager can make is delaying the decision to move someone out of their organization after it's become clear that person is a bad fit just because they are worried about leaving the role empty while they look for someone to refill that spot on their team. The second biggest mistake that a manager can make is to rush a decision to hire someone for an open role when they aren't convinced that person will be a good fit just because they are worried about leaving the role empty while they look for someone better to fill that spot on their team. Simply put, *it's far better to have an empty chair than the wrong person in the seat.*

At first, this feels very scary to most people. But, I cannot overemphasize the importance of this lesson. Just to be clear you've got it, I'll repeat—*it's far better to have an empty chair than the wrong person in the seat.* I'll admit, I don't know if I really internalized this lesson myself. Intellectually, I know that it is true. But, emotionally, in the heat of the moment when I've had to make these decisions, I've struggled with them. I've hired my second, or even third, choices for roles after my first choice turned down an offer. I've forced other hiring managers to do the same. I've kept people on staff for months after deciding they were a bad fit because I didn't think it was the right time to replace them. I've let managers keep people on staff for months because the manager argued that they needed to keep them on to finish a project even though they weren't doing a good job. I've regretted nearly all of these decisions. Whenever you're faced with a choice between an option that is difficult today and an option that will create difficulties tomorrow, choose the one that is difficult today.

At a startup, everyone feels very busy and overwhelmed all the time. This feeling will not go away. In fact, it will probably get worse as you grow. It's tempting to believe that this is because you are understaffed. This is a trap. If it was because you were understaffed, then it would not get worse as you hire more people. The truth is, you are only understaffed relative to the number of things you've decided to do. You can always just decide to do less. You can simply cross things off your to-do list by declaring them to be unimportant right now. This may sound like a bad idea. There are things that you and your management team decided to do, and now you're simply going to decide to not do them? Correct. Just don't do them. At least, don't do them right now.

There are only a handful of things that your company absolutely must do right now in order to stay in business. For example, you absolutely must make payroll. But, you don't really need full time employees to make sure you have these things covered. If push comes to shove, you can rely on external legal counsel, external financial and accounting firms, and professional employment organizations to make sure you have all of the absolute essentials covered. Everything else is discretionary. In many cases, crossing something off the to-do list will actually end up being a good thing. Most people find it hard to be as disciplined about prioritization as they should be. It's much better to do a small number of things well, than a large number of things poorly.

Moreover, there is only one person at your company who is indispensable—you. And, even then, your job as a founder is to make yourself dispensable; to build your company to the point that it doesn't need you anymore to continue on its road to success. That said, this book is aimed at early stage founders. So, you're not there yet. Remember, when your company started, it was just you. And, if absolutely necessary, it could go back to being just you again. Of course, this could be extremely painful. But, if you fear it, then your fear will cloud your judgment. General Patton said, "Any man who thinks he's indispensable, ain't." The second you start thinking that someone at your company is indispensable, slap yourself in the face and snap out of it! I don't care who it is, or what their title is!

When it comes to hiring, you should never make an offer to a candidate unless they do well on your cultural assessment, they receive stellar recommendations from their references, and you're confident they will do a great job and fit well at your company. It doesn't matter if you think the role is needed to complete a high priority project, or if you're under pressure to fill the role from your employees or even your board of directors. Leaders do not cave to pressure. In addition, you should go back to the drawing board if your first choice turns down your offer. At least, that's what you should do 90% of the time. The only exception is if you have two candidates that are essentially equal in all respects but, in particular, equal as judged by your cultural assessment. I know some leaders that, when faced with the situation of identifying two equal candidates for a role, simply hire both people. I don't think that's the right thing to do. That's a form of indecision, and indecision is a cultural anchor that will drag your company to the bottom of the sea. If your employees see you do this, they will learn that you don't think it's important to be disciplined about growing headcount, and they will learn that it's okay to take the easy way out when faced with a difficult decision. Flip a coin and make an offer.

A similar problem can happen when a candidate tells you that they have other job offers, and that you must make them an offer quickly if they are going to entertain it. This happens all the time, and you must inoculate yourself against its effects. Naturally, you will think "If this candidate has other offers, then they must be a good candidate!" However, you are building your company around yourself. Since you're unique, there is no other company like yours. Just because somebody is a great fit for another company, doesn't mean they will be a great fit for your company. So you must learn to ignore this signal. In addition, you'll likely worry that you'll have to go back to the drawing board and restart the interviewing process if you lose this candidate. This could set you back weeks, leaving your role empty for longer. Indeed, unless you were already preparing an offer for the candidate before you learned of their situation, that's exactly what you should do. Congratulate the candidate on their offer and tell them you won't be able to speed up your process. Then, go back to interviewing other candidates. An empty chair has never provided negative value.

11. Beware those with manageritis.

To borrow some phrasing from physics Nobel laureate Richard Feynman, the theoretical value of having managers in a company is offset by the general dopiness of the people who want to be managers. This dopiness is a condition I call manageritis.

In fact, if you want a first hand account of the dangers of manageritis you should read "Part 2: Mr. Feynman Goes to Washington: Investigating the Space Shuttle Challenger Disaster" in his book "What Do You Care What Other People Think". In essence, the story describes how manageritis at NASA led to the explosion of the space shuttle Challenger, killing seven astronauts, through Feynman's recounting of his investigations as part of the Presidential Commision on the disaster. He provides many examples. A common pattern in many of these examples was how the probabilities assigned to catastrophic failures of various parts of the space shuttle were decreased in various reports as they moved up the chain of command. An engineer would write a report saying that the probability of a catastrophic failure of such-and-such device was 1 in 100, then his or her manager would revise the report to say 1 in 200, and so-on and so-forth up through the layers of management until the report would come out saying that the probability of failure was in fact 1 in 100,000. And, as a result, NASA was simply declaring high risk missions to have low risk and then forging ahead. Disaster was inevitable.

Clearly, such behavior is quite bad and can be detrimental to any organization. The situation that Feynman describes at NASA seems extreme relative to my experience in industry and this extremeness is, perhaps, a symptom of the overwhelming bureaucracy and lack of accountability that seemingly characterizes government. In my experience, most managers won't blatantly lie by fudging numbers like this. However, managers in industry commonly selectively filter which information they pass up and down the chain of command. For example, as Founder and CEO, you go and tell your Vice President that there's been a development and it's crucial that they immediately drop what they've been doing and change the priorities of the teams in their organization. Then, your Vice President meets with the managers in their organization and simply says that the CEO wants them to work on a new thing. Then, the managers go and tell the individual contributors that they should spend a couple of weeks wrapping up what they've been working on, and then they will add the CEO's request to the queue of things to work on in the future. The urgency of the message gets lost as it passes through the organization, creating tremendous inertia that kills the ability of your startup to move quickly. Such behavior is very common, and also commonly happens in reverse as messages move from individual contributors, to their managers, to the Vice President, and finally to the CEO. One of my friends and colleagues has coined this "the vanishing gradient problem in organizations" in analogy with the vanishing gradient problem in deep learning, in which the magnitude of the learning signal a neural network gets from observed data decreases with each layer of neurons added to the network. In deep learning, the vanishing gradient problem is mitigated by adding skip connections, and that's how to fix it in companies too.

As a scientist, rather than a politician, Feynman just wanted to get to the truth about the proximal and ultimate causes for the failure of the Challenger. As usual, whenever he wanted to investigate a question he would be put in touch with someone in a leadership position responsible for that particular area. However, Feynman was never satisfied with the explanations he received from these bureaucrats. He wanted to get into the details, to get all the information required to draw his own conclusions rather than simply accepting the conclusions presented to him in some report. And so he would travel to the offices of the people actually designing and building the space shuttle and talk directly to the engineers himself, often spending multiple days asking them to teach him as much as they could about the technical aspects of various components or systems. Through these stories, Feynman teaches us a fundamental lesson about organizations: if you want to understand what's really going on, you need to talk directly to the individual contributors rather than managers or leadership. Therefore you, as Founder and CEO, need to talk directly to all of the individual contributors at your company all of the time.

Your startup cannot tolerate fiefdoms or fiefdom building. If any manager tries to prevent direct communication between you and the people on their team, or between the people on their team and people in other parts of the organization, you should fire them immediately. If you give them a suggestion on how to solve a problem and—rather than arguing with you about the substance of your suggestion, which is perfectly fine and to be encouraged—they dismiss your suggestion because "that's a problem for engineering to figure out" or some other nonsense about it not being within your area, you should fire them immediately. Communication across teams should be encouraged, because good ideas often come from someone with fresh eyes. Turf wars are unacceptable. Show zero tolerance for fiefdom building.

When you initially start your company there will likely be very few people working at it, and every single one of those people should report directly to you. During this stage, people probably shouldn't have normal sounding job titles at all. Instead, they should have roles like "Engineering" or "Sales" or "Operations". There's no point in introducing a hierarchy in a 10 person organization and, in fact, it is quite harmful. The company should be completely flat, with everyone reporting directly to the Founder and CEO. The point at which you decide to change this will depend on your preferences, but should probably be you have around 15 or 20 people. At that point, you can add one level to the hierarchy by adding a manager (or promoting someone to that role) in an area that is not one of your areas of comparative advantage. Everyone working in one of your areas of comparative advantage should continue to report directly to you for a while longer. Moreover, you should make it explicit that everyone—every single employee—at your startup has a "dotted line" reporting to you —forever.

Jensen Huang of NVIDIA is well known for this leadership strategy. He has an enormous number of direct reports. He does not hold regular 1-on-1s with direct reports, instead preferring to deliver all feedback during team meetings. He encourages all employees to email him their top 5 priorities each week, and he reads hundreds of these emails each morning to get a sense of what's really happening at all levels of his company.

You should create a leadership team at your company when you approach 50 people. Around this time, your company should have three levels. Individual contributors, who report to managers, who report to the CEO. Each of these managers should be a player/coach covering one area of your business. And they should be exemplary culture fits. Interestingly, research shows that people who want to be managers generally make the worst managers[1] so my advice is to choose the person in each area who is the best combination of culture fit and delivering results and promote them. However, the next move presents one of the most challenging stages in the life of a startup. This is the stage at which you add another later, which I'll call the layer of Vice Presidents. At this point, your company will look like individual contributors, who report to managers, who report to Vice Presidents, who report to the

---

1. How Do You Find a Good Manager? Ben Weidmann, Joseph Vecci, Farah Said, David J. Deming & Sonia R. Bhalotra. Working Paper 32699. DOI 10.3386/w32699. Issue Date July 2024

CEO. This is when the vanishing gradient problem really starts to rear its ugly head.

You should expect every one of your Vice Presidents to be a player/coach too. If a candidate for one of your Vice President roles ever uses the phrase "manager of managers", eliminate them from consideration immediately. If they already work at your company, fire them. Anyone I've ever met who aspired to be a "manager of managers" was a bozo. You need doers, not talkers! Your Vice Presidents should be able to drill down into the details with the individual contributors in their organization, and then zoom out to think about the entire company as part of the leadership team, and then zoom out even further to see the impact of the company's huge vision. It takes exceptional people to do this job well because they need both breadth and depth. Be very careful when recruiting these people, and take their 3 month check in very seriously. Hiring the wrong person for one of your leadership roles can hurt your company dearly and cause you a lot of pain.

A lot of people who want to become Vice President of such-and-such are interested in climbing the career ladder, of getting to higher and higher echelons of companies (but, usually not in taking the risk to start their own companies). But, you shouldn't have anyone else in your company with a C-level title until you hit approximately 100 employees. You need to keep your organization as flat as possible, as long as possible, filling all leadership and management roles with doers instead of talkers.

Even as your company grows and you add a couple (but not too many) new layers of management, actually especially as this happens, you need to keep talking directly with the individual contributors at your company every single day. You must stay in the details within your areas of comparative advantage. In fact, I would suggest that you continue to dedicate at least 40% of your time as an individual contributor within your areas of comparative advantage. This amounts to two days per week of individual contributor work. That way, you never lose touch with what's really going on at your company.

Aside from actually taking part in projects as an individual contributor, I tried two methods for communicating with everyone at my company. The first was question-and-answer style town halls, both with the whole company and with randomly chosen subsets. Without question, I found that the town halls with randomly chosen subsets of people generated better questions and more conversation than those with the whole company because the smaller group makes it more conversational. However, the drawback is that not everyone is present and able to hear what was said. So, it's a good idea to record these town halls, either on video or as a transcript. I do not believe you should use a tool that lets people submit written questions for the town hall, especially anonymously. You might think that anonymity encourages people to ask the hard hitting, important questions, but actually it encourages them to ask the stupidest possible questions such as why you don't provide their favorite flavor of sparkling water in the fridge. Town halls should be back-and-forth conversations between you and people that work at your company, looking each other in the eye and using your voices the old fashioned way. The second method I tried was having 1-on-1s with randomly chosen people a few times a week, usually just over Slack. Essentially, these started with "Hey, how's it going this week?" or something like that, with the goal of drilling down into what they were working on and where they needed help moving things forward. I found these random 1-on-1s to be useful, but I think Jensen's strategy is better. Just have everyone send you a list of their top 5 priorities each week, and then randomly choose a subset of those to dig in deeper on.

The precursor to the US Central Intelligence Agency, the Office of Strategic Services or OSS, published a document called the "Simple Sabotage Field Manual" in 1944 during World War 2. Of particular interest for our purposes is a section of this document called "General Interference with Organizations and Production" that outlines a set of tactics a saboteur may employ to disrupt an organization (like a company) from the inside out. At the very beginning of this document, it says "[t]he contents of this Manual should be carefully controlled and should not be allowed to come into unauthorized hands" but clearly this has failed, because it seems from the behavior of those with manageritis that they are teaching it in business schools as the proper way to operate as a manager.

Here are some of the highlights:

- Make speeches. Talk as frequently as possible and at great length.

- Hold conferences and meetings when there is more critical work to be done.
- Insist on doing everything through "proper channels". Never permit short-cuts to be taken in order to expedite decisions.
- When possible, refer all matters to committees for further study and consideration. Attempt to make the committees as large as possible—never fewer than five people.
- Multiply the procedures and clearances involved in making decisions. See that three people have to approve everything where one would do.
- Refer back to matters decided upon at the last meeting and attempt to re-open the question of the advisability of that decision.
- Advocate caution. Be "reasonable" and urge your colleagues to "be reasonable" and avoid haste which might result in embarrassments or difficulties later on. Apply all regulations to the last letter.
- Bring up irrelevant issues as frequently as possible, and haggle over the precise wordings of communications, minutes, resolutions.
- Misunderstand directions. Ask endless questions or engage in long correspondence about the strategy. Quibble over minor tactical details whenever you can.
- Always assign the unimportant jobs first, and see that the important jobs are assigned to inefficient workers.
- To lower morale and with it, production, be pleasant to inefficient workers; give them undeserved promotions. Discriminate against efficient workers; complain unjustly about their work.

If you have any experience working in industry, especially at large corporations, I'd bet that many of these items sound quite familiar to you. You need to make sure you do not have any managers at your company who are inadvertently sabotaging you.

When I discussed promotions in an earlier chapter, I mentioned that you should have a clearly stated policy that three conditions must be met for anyone to be promoted (i) you must have an open role at a more senior level, (ii) the internal candidate must have demonstrated that they are great culture fit, and (iii) the internal candidate must have delivered outstand results in their current role. A promotion can, and should usually, mean taking on more responsibility as an individual contributor; not taking on management responsibilities. You should be very wary of hiring people into your company who express that they want to be managers, because they are most commonly afflicted by manageritis. People who state that they want to be managers generally make worse managers than randomly chosen people. [2] In fact, there are primarily two attributes that predict if someone may be a good manager: their fluid intelligence (the ability to think abstractly, reason, and solve problems without relying on prior knowledge) and their ability to make decisions. Delivering outstanding results in a good proxy for these, so only promote proven doers who can deliver outstanding results while exemplifying your cultural principles.

---

2. https://www.nber.org/papers/w32699

12. Only wimps whine about psychological safety.

Psychological safety refers to an environment in which individuals feel comfortable expressing their thoughts, questions, concerns, or mistakes without fear of negative consequences such as ridicule, rejection, or punishment. In principle, this sounds like a good thing, to be encouraged, maybe even nurtured within an organization. Certainly, you want people at your company taking risks, running experiments, and trying new things—most of which will not work—because that is the key to innovation. That is, you want people to make mistakes and to learn from those mistakes. Of course, at the same time you cannot make too many mistakes or your company will go out of business. So you must find a balance. Certainly, you also want people to speak up and say what's on their mind, to express their opinions, to point out when something has gone wrong and offer suggestions for how to fix it. Both of those things make sense on their own. But, they lead to an interesting contradiction: do you want someone to speak up when they think somebody else is making a mistake?

Imagine you have two employees, Alice and Bob. If Alice believes that Bob is making a mistake—maybe even a big mistake—and speaks up about it she could be infringing on Bob's sense of psychological safety. Bob could feel that he is not free to make mistakes and learn from them. On the other hand, if Alice is not free to speak up when she thinks Bob is making a mistake, then she doesn't have psychological safety because she is not able to express her honest thoughts and opinions. So, what do you do?

Safetyism, as discussed by Jonathan Haidt and Greg Lukianoff in their book The Coddling of the American Mind, refers to an overemphasis on protecting individuals from emotional discomfort, potentially at the expense of exposure to diverse ideas and resilience-building experiences. This is exemplified by requests to include "trigger warnings" before presentations that include certain types of content, attempts to suppress others' freedom of speech or censor the expression of "triggering" topics, and calls to "cancel" people for simply expressing their ideas and opinions. The contradiction is obvious—I can only feel safe if you don't feel safe, so in the name of safety you must be made to feel unsafe. It's a catch-22.

Although the concept of psychological safety in the workplace is generally good, its interaction with the rise of safetyism in general could be disastrous for those trying to build ambitious startups or incredible products. Safetyism creates a race to the bottom, in which an organization must bend to the will of its most neurotic members. But great things are born out of productive conflict, not in spite of it.

Steve Jobs once told the following story in an interview:

"When I was a young kid there was a widowed man that lived up the street. He was in his eighties. He was a little scary looking. And I got to know him a little bit. I think he may have paid me to mow his lawn or something.

One day he said to me, 'Come on into my garage, I want to show you something.' And he pulled out this dusty old rock tumbler. It was a motor and a coffee can and a little band between them. And he said, 'Come with me.' We went out into the back and we got just some rocks... some regular old ugly rocks. And we put them in the can with a little bit of liquid and a little bit of grit powder, and we closed the can up and he turned this motor on and he said, 'come back tomorrow.'

And this can was making a racket as the stones went around.

And I came back the next day, and we opened the can. And we took out these amazingly beautiful polished rocks. The same common stones that had gone in, through rubbing against each other like this (Jobs clapped his hands), creating a little bit of friction, creating a little bit of noise, had come out these beautiful polished rocks.

That's always been in my mind my metaphor for a team working really hard on something they're passionate about."

I've always thought this was a beautiful metaphor for explaining what a good startup culture looks like, and I've used it many times to illustrate that conflict is a key prerequisite to greatness. If, in order to prevent emotional discomfort in yourself or others, you avoid throwing the rocks into the rock tumbler, then they never get polished.

I believe that two things must happen simultaneously in order to create an environment in which people generally experience psychological safety.

First, you should only hire people who are naturally prone to feeling psychologically safe. Resilient, adaptable people who are not put off by conflict will tend to feel psychologically safe in any environment. Rocks that are made from the right materials can be polished by hitting each other, but rocks made from the wrong materials will crack and break.

High-agency individuals are generally less prone to feeling a lack of psychological safety, largely because their strong sense of control, resilience, and confidence can buffer them against the external environment's uncertainties. Their belief in their own ability to navigate challenges means they often experience less anxiety over things they can't control and are more focused on their capacity to affect outcomes. In contrast, individuals with lower agency may feel more reliant on external validation or support, which can make them more sensitive to criticism or unpredictable situations, affecting their psychological safety. This reliance often makes a culture of safety and support critical for them to thrive.

Indeed, psychological research suggests that people who have high agreeableness or high neuroticism are more prone to experiencing psychological distress in the workplace than those who are lower in those personality traits. [1] Back when I grew up in the 90s, we would have called such people "wimps". If you simply do not hire wimps, then you are well on your way to creating an environment in which your team members experience psychological safety. If you hire people who feel psychological safety in almost any environment, then they are likely to feel psychologically safe in your work environment. In addition, research shows that personality alignment between a manager and their direct reports promotes feelings of psychological safety. This is a key reason why I've put so much emphasis on cultural principles and on assessing culture fit during the hiring process.

Second, create a culture in which people offer suggestions when they point out potential problems instead of just complaining about them. This is what I call productive conflict. In reflecting about the culture he observed at NASA, Professor Feynman drew a contrast with the culture he observed at Los Alamos as part of the Manhattan Project where he "experienced the tension and pressure of everybody working together to make the atomic bomb." Feynman noted,

"When somebody is having a problem, say with the detonator, everybody knows that it's a big problem. They're thinking of ways to beat it. They're making suggestions. And when they hear about the solution, they're excited. Because that means their work is now useful. If the detonator didn't work, the bomb wouldn't work. I figured the same thing had gone on at NASA in the early days [of the moon landing]. If the spacesuit

---

1. https://www.ncbi.nlm.nih.gov/pmc/articles/PMC8705123/

didn't work, they couldn't go to the moon. So everybody is interested in everybody else's problems.

It's not a question of what has been written down, or who should tell what to whom, it's a question of whether when you do tell somebody about some problem they're delighted to hear about it and they say 'tell me more!' and 'have you tried such-and-such?' or they say 'well, see what you can do about it!' which is a completely different atmosphere [than NASA]."

Everybody makes mistakes. This is especially true at startups, where a common analogy is that you're building the plane as you're flying it. Your employees will make mistakes. Your board members will make mistakes. You—perhaps most of all—will make mistakes. As long as you still have cash in the bank, every mistake you make that doesn't kill you makes you stronger. Try to create a culture like the one Feynman attributes to Los Alamos; one in which nobody is worried about speaking up about mistakes or problems, and nobody is worried that someone will point out their mistakes or the problems they've caused, because nobody is ever complaining, instead they are all working together to achieve the vision. Alice says to Bob, "Hey Bob, I don't think your method is going to work. Have you tried such-and-such instead?", and Bob replies, "I'm not convinced, give me another day to see if my method will work." or "Hmm ... I think you may be right, Alice. Let's give such-and-such a try." Alice isn't afraid to speak her mind, Bob isn't offended by it, and the company is stronger as a result. That's a productive conflict.

At the same time, you are running a business and are account-able for results to your customers and to financial results for your investors, so you cannot tolerate all types of mistakes. There are four types of mistakes that you cannot tolerate. The first type includes things that are illegal, violate some important regulation, or create a serious legal liability for the company. The second type includes mistakes with big consequences that are essentially irreversible, like someone accidentally deleting the only copy of a movie you've been working on for years (which nearly happened at Pixar). The third type includes mistakes that take too long to uncover, often because the person in charge of the project is unwilling to admit that they've made a mistake. Spending months on a doomed project after it seemed likely that it was doomed is a very bad mistake, because you can't get that time back and time is of the essence for a startup. The fourth type includes repeated mistakes, because if someone is repeating the same mistake over and over again then they are either incapable or unwilling to learn. Any type of mistake that doesn't fall into one of these four categories is perfectly fine.

If your startup is going to be successful, you will require an employee base with a high tolerance for stressful, ambiguous situations who can self-motivate and push through odds stacked against them. You want ambitious people motivated by impact rather than people looking for a fun, easy-going work environment. The "startup special forces"—highly capable individuals with a strong bias towards action and results, who need minimal oversight and aren't phased by change or uncertainty. These are people who can function between and across teams, be shifted from project to project on a whim, and who put the company mission above all else. People who look at a seemingly insurmountable obstacle and shout "let's fucking go" as they charge ahead together. If you fill your company with people like that, nobody will whine about psychological safety, because they'll have the agency to create it for themselves.

13. Grade A treatment for A-players.

If you follow the suggestions in the previous chapters, you'll have created a process by which it's very difficult for someone to earn a spot on your team. First, a job candidate must self-assess that they align with your company's vision and cultural principles. Next, they must go through a multi-step interview process in which they must pass a resume-blinded cultural assessment and a 1.5 hour long live skills assessment in which they give a presentation on a relevant technical topic and get peppered with questions from experts on your team. Then, they need to receive great reviews from 2-3 references, both in terms of their ability to do the job and their alignment with your company's cultural principles. Finally, they need to perform well on a peer assessment after 90 days on the job to see how well they are performing and how strongly they fit the company's culture. In addition, you should approach each step in this process so that a candidate must check all of the boxes in order to move forward, and that failing to check even a single box disqualifies them from further consideration. You should expect high attrition rates at each step of the interview process, and you should even expect up to 30% of new hires to fail their 90 day assessment. This is a process designed to only let A-players through, which means that once they are through, you should treat them like A-players.

I'm not sure if there is a universal definition of what it means to be treated like an A-player. It's possible that the way A-players want to be treated could vary by industry, or it may differ between companies with different cultural principles. So, you're going to have to do some research on this and come up with your own ideas. But, I do have a few suggestions.

First, A-players are top tier talent and should be compensated appropriately. At a startup, they should be given equity in the company (usually granted as options to purchase shares in the future) in addition to a salary. Some startups also offer cash bonuses for performance, especially for sales roles which often include a substantial component as variable compensation. I recommend using market data to guide your compensation practices. You can find data on compensation at startups from providers like Carta and others. You will be able to filter by industry, size of company, and role, and should try to match these to your company as closely as possible. Then, target a percentile of the distribution of total compensation such as the 80th or 90th percentile—remember these are A-players who've made it through a tough interview process! Use this as a guideline for setting the total salary, equity, and bonus compensation. How you choose to break that up depends on your company, but I suggest leaning more heavily on equity based compensation in the early days; both because your company likely doesn't have that much cash in the early days, and because most A-players will be attracted by the opportunity to have an ownership stake in your company. In addition, offer good health insurance benefits and a 401(k) (if you can afford it). As a small early stage startup, it's often easiest to provide benefits through Professional Employer Organization (PEO) like TriNet, Justworks, or Rippling. These organizations act to pool the employees across many small companies in order to gain access to better benefits at lower rates, and their platforms simplify benefit administration and payroll. Often, startups switch from using a PEO for benefits administration and payroll to doing these activities themselves when they reach around 100 employees.

Next, I believe that you and your leadership team should share essentially all information with all employees (that is, those who have passed their 90-day assessment)—total transparency. Nearly anything that can be discussed with your leadership team can, and should, be shared with the entire company openly and honestly. Patent applications? Share them. Financial metrics? Share them. Key performance indicators? Share them. The only exceptions to this are topics where sharing the information would violate someone's privacy or create liability for the company. Some leaders don't like to share bad news with employees because they are worried it will affect morale. Similarly, some leaders don't like to let their employees follow along during discussions that will lead to important decisions because they think the uncertainty of a looming big decision will scare them. In my opinion, these leaders don't have respect for their employees! If your employees are really A-players then bad news or uncertainty won't negatively affect their morale, in fact, quite the opposite—a team of A-players will proactively lean in to help you and your leadership team solve these problems. They will rally to the cause.

Finally, most A-players are motivated by the opportunity to make an impact. They have signed up to come work for your company because they care about the vision. So let them make an impact! Let them experiment! Let them try new things and new ideas! Let them fail! Then, let them try again with a new approach! As long an employee is aligned with your vision, embodies your cultural principles, realizes their mistakes quickly, and learns from those mistakes so they don't repeat them—that is, they are an A-player—then you can point them in the direction of a mountain top and let them sprint their way to the summit. Not only that, but A-players will hold each other accountable so that you don't have to micromanage everyone. In addition, remember that most people like to celebrate their wins. In football, when a player makes a big play or scores a touchdown they get high fives from their teammates. When they win a big game, they dump a bucket of gatorade on the coach. And, if they win the Super Bowl, they throw a parade. Come up with some rituals like this to help your team celebrate or, better yet, let your team come up with some themselves.

Note that I'm not saying that you should stop getting your hands dirty within your areas of comparative advantage. Any employee who wants you to stop doing that is engaging in a turf war, creating a fiefdom, and is not an A-player. A-players will welcome your involvement and collaboration. Nor am I saying that you shouldn't hold everyone to a high standard, that you should accept the results that people send your way as good enough. Instead, you must challenge everyone to do their best possible work—no, to do work that is even better than they thought was possible. Your team of A-players will rise to the occasion.

These three suggestions—high compensation, full transparency, focusing on impact—are great ways to motivate A-players, but are terrible ideas on a team with B-players. With a team of B-players, you'll need more people to match the output of a team of A-players and paying them a lot will bankrupt your company as a result. B-players will freeze in the headlights when there is bad news or uncertainty, rather than rallying to the cause like A-players. B-players will hesitate, dilly dally, or get lost if you simply point them at the summit of the mountain, unlike A-players who will find their way to the top on their own. If you start letting B-players into your company, all of these things that work so well for A-players will start to backfire. So, you can only do these things if you are truly serious about letting the right ones in and moving the wrong ones out.

A final observation is that A-players don't really give a shit about most of the stupid perks that many technology companies offer these days. They don't care if your company has a ping pong table or kombucha on top. A-players mostly care about being on a team with other A-players because they want to make an impact and work to advance an ambitious vision. Therefore, I don't think it's a good idea to offer lots of stupid tech company perks—those things are just bait for B-players.

14. What do you care what investors think?

Most entrepreneurs should not raise venture capital. Especially not at an early stage. It's usually better to bootstrap your company by generating revenue immediately. This allows you to grow at the right pace, and to maintain control of your company for as long as possible. Sometimes, once you are seeing strong traction and revenue growth, it may make sense to raise venture capital for a previously bootstrapped company so that you can invest in ways to accelerate that growth. In my opinion, there is only one good exception to this rule, which is if you are starting a "deep tech" company. A startup belongs to the class of deep tech companies if it requires substantial up front investment in engineering or research and development. Examples include companies involved in areas like biotechnology, quantum computing, robotics, nuclear energy, or space exploration. It is generally impossible to build a deep tech company without a lot of capital, and venture capital firms are often the best source. Given that this book is aimed at "ambitious" founders with huge visions, the intended audience includes lots of deep tech founders like myself. I raised around $135M in venture capital for my first startup, and this chapter describes many of the (somewhat contrarian) lessons I learned along the way.

Regardless of the type of company you're aiming to start, venture investors will only be interested if it has the potential to be a multi-billion dollar business. That's not a contrarian belief; any venture investor will say the same. If your company doesn't have that potential, or it's not something you want to try for, then you should not raise venture capital. If that means you can't start your company for some reason, then don't. In some areas, like biotechnology, investors may invest a large amount of capital at the start and, as a result, own a large fraction of the business from the beginning. In most areas, however, investors will purchase shares in successive rounds of financing often called Seed, Series A, Series B, etc. Investors are typically looking to realize a return on their investment after approximately 10 years, which means they will want the company to exit by going public or selling to another business around that point in time. If you've sold a controlling stake in your company at that point, you will not have a choice. The instant you've sold a controlling stake in your company, it is no longer your company.

As a general rule of thumb, your company will need to be generating at least $100M in revenue each year with a high rate of growth (e.g., 50% year-over-year) in order to have a chance for an attractive exit. The specific requirements vary a lot depending on market conditions and industry, and evolve over time, so just treat those numbers as an order-of-magnitude rule-of-thumb. In any case, if you choose to take on venture capital, that's the type of expectations you are signing yourself up for. You must build a strong business generating substantial annual revenue, that's also growing quickly, and that has the potential to get much, much bigger in the future. And they'll expect you to do this in 10 years. The nightmare scenario for most venture investors isn't that your company goes out of business, it's that it does well enough to stay in business but doesn't do well enough to merit a big exit. If you build a business making $50M a year profitably so that it could be self-sustaining, there's a good chance you'll find yourself getting acquired by a private equity firm so that your investors can get liquidity. From what I hear, this will be the least fun experience you'll have in your whole life—private equity firms have the worst reputation for treating people like shit. Venture backed founders are not in the business of hitting singles or doubles, they are in the grand slam business. Make sure you know what *you* want before you step up to the plate.

If you still want to raise venture capital after reading the introduction—perhaps you are starting a deep tech company (and I hope so, because I believe deep tech companies are a great way to help move society forward)—then here is a non-exhaustive list of a few key terms you should know.

Lead Investor

A lead investor is the primary investor in a funding round who sets the terms of the investment and often contributes a significant portion of the capital. They negotiate the term sheet with your company, perform due diligence, and may help attract other investors to complete the round. The lead investor might secure a seat on your board of directors, providing guidance and influence over strategic decisions. Having a reputable lead investor can lend credibility and streamline the fundraising process, but it's important to ensure their interests align with yours and that the terms are fair.

Term Sheet

A *term sheet* is a summary of the proposed investment deal. It's a non-binding document that outlines the main terms and conditions of the investment. It includes details about the valuation, investment amount, and the percentage of the company the investor will own. The term sheet also specifies any special rights the investor will have, such as a seat on the board or specific voting rights, and any conditions that need to be met before the deal is finalized. It's usually very short, just one page or so. If someone gives you a term sheet much longer than that, run away quickly. You can negotiate the terms with an investor by marking up the term sheet with track changes and sending it back, which is called a redline (your lawyer will do this).

Convertible Note

A *convertible note* is an agreement where an investor lends money to your company with the expectation that this loan will turn into shares of your company in the future. The investor provides funds, and initially, this money is considered a loan that collects interest over time. Instead of repaying the loan with interest, you and the investor agree that the loan will convert into shares of your company at a later date or during a particular event, typically during your next major funding round. Convertible notes often include terms like a valuation cap and a discount rate, which can give the investor a better deal when the loan converts into shares. Convertible notes are popular instruments for investments in early stage companies because they don't require the parties to commit to a valuation at the time of the investment; instead, the valuation at which the loan converts into shares is determined by the minimum of the valuation in the next priced equity round or the valuation cap of the note. If you fail to raise another equity round and cannot meet the terms of the loan agreement, your company may have to default and could go into bankruptcy. It's generally not a good idea to raise multiple rounds in a row as convertible notes, which people call stacking convertible notes. Unless you really know what you're doing, and if you're a first time founder you should assume that you do not, don't stack convertible notes.

SAFE (Simple Agreement for Future Equity)

A *SAFE* is similar to a convertible note but a bit simpler and, supposedly, more founder friendly. It's an agreement where an investor gives you money now in exchange for the right to receive shares in your company later, usually during your next significant funding round. Unlike convertible notes, SAFEs aren't loans, so there's no interest to worry about, and you don't have to deal with maturity dates or repayment terms. With a SAFE, the investor will get shares when you next sell equity in your company. The agreement may include a valuation cap or a discount, just like a convertible note, which can offer the investor a better deal when converting to shares. SAFEs are considered founder-friendly because they're straightforward and eliminate the complexities of debt or interest. They are cost-effective and quick to arrange due to their simplicity, making them an attractive option for early-stage startups seeking rapid funding.

Valuation Cap

Convertible and SAFE notes don't typically specify a valuation for a company. Instead, the initial investment converts into shares at the minimum of the next round's price or a *valuation cap*. It ensures that early investors get a fair share of your company in exchange for being really early, even if your company's value increases significantly later on. For example, imagine you receive $100,000 from an investor with a valuation cap of $5 million. Later, when your company is valued at $10 million, the investor's loan converts to shares as if your company were worth $5 million (the cap). This means the investor gets more shares than they would have if the conversion were based on the $10 million valuation, giving them a larger share of the company. Founders of particularly hot early stage startups can sometimes command uncapped notes, usually with terms that specify the note will convert into shares at a discount relative to the price of the next round.

Pre-Money Valuation

Pre-money valuation is the value of your company before new investments come in. It's the starting point for figuring out how much of your company you need to give to new investors. For example, suppose your company's pre-money valuation is $4 million, and an investor wants to invest $1 million. The post-money valuation becomes $5 million (pre-money valuation plus the investment amount). The investor's ownership percentage is calculated by dividing their investment by the post-money valuation: $1 million divided by $5 million equals 20%. This means the investor will own 20% of your company after the investment. Personally, I've always found it easier to reason about post-money valuations, but it's important to know both terms.

Post-Money Valuation

Post-money valuation is your company's value after receiving the investment. It is calculated by adding the pre-money valuation and the investment amount. This figure is significant because it determines everyone's ownership percentages after the investment and shows how much existing owners' shares are diluted. The calculation above in the definition of pre-money valuation should explain the concept.

Dilution

Dilution occurs anytime new shares are issued by the company, which reduces the ownership percentage of existing share-holders. There are a variety of reasons a company may issue new shares, but a common reason is to raise capital. When you raise money from a venture capital firm as part of a priced equity round, the investor is actually purchasing new shares that will be issued by your company. For example, suppose your company has 1M shares. Then, you raise $2M at a $10M post-money valuation. Your company will issue 250,000 new shares (usually as preferred shares which have more rights than the common shares that founders and employees typi-cally receive) and deliver them to the investor. Thus, the investor will end up owning 250,000 out of 1,250,000 shares, or 20% of the company. If you and your co-founders owned all 1M shares prior to the investment round, amounting to 100%

of the company, after the round closes you will still own 1M shares but it will only amount to 80% of the company because the company has issued additional shares. Dilution can impact control over company decisions if your ownership percentage decreases significantly, so it's important to be aware of dilution and consider ways to protect your ownership stake. The simplest way is to raise as little capital is needed to build your company.

Common and Preferred Shares

Common and preferred shares are two types of equity that represent ownership in a company, but they come with different rights and privileges. Common shares are the basic units of ownership in a company. Holders of common shares have voting rights, allowing them to vote on important company matters such as electing the board of directors or approving significant corporate actions. However, common shareholders are last in line when it comes to receiving dividends or assets if the company is liquidated. This means if the company goes bankrupt or is sold, common shareholders receive payouts only after all debts and obligations to creditors and preferred shareholders are satisfied. Founders and employees typically hold common shares. Preferred shares offer certain advantages over common shares. Preferred shareholders usually receive dividends before common shareholders and have priority in asset distribution if the company is liquidated. In venture capital deals, investors often receive preferred shares to protect their investments. These shares often come with some special rights which are beyond the scope of this book, and you should discuss any of these terms with your legal counsel during negotiation of a term sheet.

Stock Options

Stock options are contracts that grant employees the right, but not the obligation, to purchase a certain number of company shares at a predetermined price, known as the strike price or exercise price, after a specified vesting period. The exercise price of an option in a startup is estimated based on the company's value through a process called 409A valuation that you can obtain from an accredited appraiser such as Carta. Typically, stock options vest over time, meaning employees earn the right to exercise their options gradually. A common vesting schedule is four years with a one-year cliff. This means that after one year of employment, 25% of the options vest, and the remaining 75% vest monthly over the next three years. Vesting incentivizes employees to stay with the company longer and align their interests with the company's success. You will typically set aside a pool of equity to grant to new employees as stock options. The size of this pool is often increased when you raise capital to ensure there are sufficient equity incentives for new employees, and the size of the new pool would be described in the term sheet.

Board Seats

A board seat refers to a position on a company's board of directors, the governing body responsible for overseeing the company's management and providing guidance on significant strategic decisions. Often, the board of directors at a startup will just be the company's founders when it is first incorporated. The lead investor in a round of financing will often request a seat on the company's board of directors as a condition of their investment. In other cases, investors making a substantial financial commitment may request a role as a board observer. A board observer is entitled to attend board meetings and to all information the company provides to the board of directors, but they are not able to vote as a typical board member. A startup board typically includes three to seven board members, and usually includes founders, investors, and independent directors who are recruited to serve on the board (but don't represent the founders or the investors). The board of directors will vote on various issues, such as whether or not the company should accept a term sheet for a new investment, either through an in-person vote at a board meeting or via a unanimous written consent prepared by your legal counsel. Startup boards typically meet quarterly.

You'll encounter people with all kinds of titles when you start talking to venture capital firms in order to raise money for your startup. It's confusing. Here's a short guide to many of the common titles in venture capital firms.

Analyst

Analysts are usually early in their VC careers and are responsible for sourcing deals, conducting market research, and supporting the investment team. They might be your first point of contact and can help champion your startup internally.

Associate

Associates are a step up from analysts and often have more experience. They assist in evaluating investment opportunities, performing due diligence, and may have some say in investment decisions. They can be helpful allies in getting your deal in front of the partners.

Principal

Principals are senior members who play a significant role in deal sourcing, evaluation, and execution. They often have the authority to make investment recommendations and may lead deals, but usually need partner approval for final decisions.

Vice President (VP)

VPs are similar to principals, with substantial responsibilities in sourcing and managing investments. They may have more influence over investment decisions and often work closely with portfolio companies post-investment.

Partner

Partners are key decision-makers in the firm. They have the authority to approve investments and usually sit on the boards of portfolio companies. Partners are the ones who can write the check, so building a relationship with them is crucial.

Managing Partner or General Partner (GP)

Managing Partners or General Partners are at the top of the firm's hierarchy. They oversee the firm's strategy, fundraising, and major investment decisions. They have significant influence and make final calls on investments.

Venture Partner

Venture Partners are typically experienced entrepreneurs or executives who work with the firm on a part-time basis. They help source deals and may work closely with portfolio companies but might not be involved in the firm's day-to-day operations.

Operating Partner

Operating Partners focus on helping portfolio companies grow by providing operational expertise. They might assist with scaling, hiring, or strategy execution but are less involved in making investment decisions.

Entrepreneur-in-Residence (EIR)

EIRs are seasoned entrepreneurs temporarily affiliated with the VC firm. They're often exploring their next venture or assisting the firm with deal sourcing and due diligence. While not decision-makers, they can be helpful for networking or, if you build a good relationship, as a coach given that they've started companies before.

In order to raise capital, you'll usually need to share information with potential investors using the following things.

Non-confidential Pitch Deck

A non-confidential pitch deck is a presentation you share with potential investors to give them an overview of your startup without revealing any sensitive information. It should be short, something you could run through in 15 minutes. And it should tell a story! It covers the basics like your vision, market opportunity, business model, and team. Do not share financial information in this deck. Think of it as your startup's highlight reel meant to intrigue investors without going into too many details. You could share this deck as part of a first meeting, but only while you are actively fundraising. Many investors will ask you to share a deck even while you aren't actively fundraising, and you should refuse.

Confidential Pitch Deck

A confidential pitch deck dives deeper into your startup and includes information you'd only share under a non-disclosure agreement (NDA). This version might contain details about your proprietary technology, customers, or financials. Investors will definitely want you to share information about your current financials and projections. I view the confidential deck as an appendix of supporting information for your non-confidential deck. It's less story, more facts and analysis. You should only share this deck in a second meeting with an investor, after they've signed an NDA. I recommend putting a watermark on it to make it clear that the deck is confidential, because many investors will share your deck with others even when you ask them not to.

Financial Model

A financial model is a spreadsheet that projects your company's financial performance over the next few years. There are some fancy apps for making startup financial models, don't use them. Investors just want this in Excel format. It includes your assumptions about revenue growth, expenses, cash flow, and other key metrics. Building one forces you to think through how your business will make money and helps investors understand your financial plans. It's basically showing the math behind your vision, proving that you've thought about the numbers and not just the big ideas. At least, that's what some people think. In reality, a financial model for an early stage startup is just a guess. You shouldn't worry about making exact projections, you're just trying to estimate the order of magnitude; is this a $10M per year business, a $100M per year business, or a $1B per year business? You should give your financial model to interested investors at the same time as you give them your confidential deck. Any investor who makes a big deal of needed exact projections, or expects you to hit these projections going forward like a public company, when your startup is still at an early stage is a mutual fund manager cosplaying as a venture capitalist. Politely tell them to go pound sand, then go look for another investor with a damn backbone.

Data Room

A data room is a secure online folder where you keep all the important documents that investors might ask for during due diligence. This includes things like incorporation documents, financial statements, cap tables, contracts, employee agreements, minutes for board meetings, and any other legal or financial paperwork. Having a well-organized data room makes it easier for investors to review your company and shows that you're prepared and transparent. Your legal counsel can advise you on how to set this up.

These are the "normal things" that investors will expect you to share with them. Personally, I don't like the use of slide decks for conveying information. Slides should only be used as tools to accompany a presentation by a speaker, and they shouldn't make sense without the voice over. A written memo is a much better way to convey information. So, I suggest writing a three-to-five page memo on your vision and why your startup is going to be the one to realize it. This is a great thing to share with potential investors at any time. Hell, you can even publish it on a blog or something, along with your secret plan, if you feel so inclined. Unfortunately, people with manageritis love slide decks and hate memos, probably because their brains have largely turned off. The reading is just too much for them, perhaps. And, lots of people with manageritis become investors after working at some stupid consulting firm like McKinsey, where they are thoroughly infected by the disease. So, it may be difficult for you to avoid using both the deck and memo if you're running a broad fundraising process.

I banned slide presentations during the first few years of Unlearn's existence. No slides were ever used for any internal meetings. Ever. Instead, the leader of the meeting would prepare a three page, narrative structured memo for everyone to read at the start of the meeting. Then, we would revise the memo based on the outcome of the meeting. Some of you may recognize this as Amazon's memo policy. It's effective, both as a communication and a cultural tool.

Slides aren't inherently evil. They are a useful tool to accompany a presentation given by an enthusiastic, engaging speaker. But, in my opinion, people aren't taught how to use them effectively in the same way they're taught to write. As a result, almost 99% of the presentations I've seen over the years have been absolutely terrible. A waste of time. An insult to the audience. You will have to give presentations in order to raise capital, and your presentations have be fucking great if you're going to do it successfully.

Many people mistakenly believe that the primary purpose of a presentation is to inform the audience about some topic. That shit's boring. Nobody has the attention span for a crappy presentation that lists a bunch of facts in bullet points. No, the primary purpose of a presentation is to *entertain*. If you cannot keep your audience entertained and engaged throughout your presentation, then you cannot inform them of anything because they'll fall half asleep.

A presentation is essentially a visual essay, designed to persuade, and must revolve around a single big idea. In writing, we call this a "thesis sentence". We all learned to write essays focused around a clear, concise, and actionable thesis sentence, and to structure our argument into a beginning, middle, and end. Probably wrote a hundred essays like this in school. But, unfortunately, we're not taught to do that with slides.

Here are a few tips for using slides more effectively that apply to fundraising, of course, but also more broadly.

First, decide whether you need slides at all. Hell, maybe you don't even need a meeting! If you're just informing someone of something, or documenting something—providing information rather than persuading—just send an email or something.

Second, focus your presentation on three or fewer people in your audience you want to persuade. They're the key opinion leaders of your meeting. Ideally, these are real people. For example, in a pitch to an investor you want to convince both the partner you're working with, and the managing partner of the firm. However, you can also make up people if you're giving a presentation to an audience you don't yet know. Write down what you think each person's point of view will be walking into the meeting, and what you want it to be walking out.

This gives your meeting a result, a criterion for success. It's successful if it persuades the key people in your audience to leave the room with the desired point of view, but if that doesn't happen then it was not successful. The purpose of your presentation is to change people's minds about something. In the case of fundraising, you need to convince them that they should invest in your company because you have a huge vision, and you have what it takes to go out there and make it real.

Third, right down a thesis sentence for your presentation. Make it clear, concise, and actionable. It's okay if you need two or three sentences, as long as it's clear, concise, and actionable!

(Don't be afraid to repeat important ideas in your presentation!)

Finally, structure your presentation into a beginning, middle, and end. Craft each section to persuade the audience of some sub-idea, guiding them towards leaving the room with your desired point of view.

For example, my presentations are often structured as "problem, delusion, solution". In the beginning, I will describe a problem with the world today. In the middle, I take aim at a false belief I want my audience to reject. Then, in the end I present my solution and what it will do for the world.

For example, here's an outline I used for some presentations at Unlearn.

Beginning: Clinical trials are time consuming and expensive because they require so many participants, half of whom are randomly assigned to a control group in which they often receive a placebo.

Middle: Eliminating the control group could solve these problems, while better aligning trials with the goals of participants (i.e., getting access to a new drug that could help them). Unfortunately, this is a false belief because it's not possible to do without biasing the result of the trial, so medical regulators don't usually let you do it.

End: By using artificial intelligence to predict control outcomes for individual patients, we can design randomized trials that use smaller control groups without biasing the result. These trials are more efficient, but just as reliable as before.

There are a few other frameworks that can be useful for structuring your presentations like the hero's journey[1] or the audience transformation roadmap[2]. In fact, I've used both of these frameworks for various presentations. I suggest trying them out and seeing what works for you. As an aside, I'll often go through ten or more versions of a presentation before I think it's any good at all. The second version is usually a complete rewrite of the first. Sometimes the third is another complete rewrite. Then, it's usually more incremental changes after that. The point is, giving good presentations is difficult and requires lots of experimentation.

------

1. Resonate by Nancy Duarte.
2. https://www.ideasonstage.com/communication-consulting/audience-trans formation-roadmap/

None of these tips so far has anything to do with the visuals on your slides, only the global structure of the presentation. This is all prep work you should do before even opening your presentation software, just ideating at a white board.

In terms of visuals, I recommend having an agenda slide that you periodically repeat between sections to help prepare the audience for the next sub-idea. Actually, this is really to help you remember what you're going to say next and to stop you from rushing through your slides. Also, use a much bigger font than you think you should—like size 36 or something. It will force you to be more concise. Think through every graph, bullet point, figure, slide, etc; if it isn't absolutely necessary for conveying your big idea and persuading your audience, delete it. Each slide should have only a few words on it and a picture that's very interesting but that can be understood by your audience in a few seconds so that it doesn't distract them from what you're saying. You are the center of attention, not your slides. Use contrast and animations to guide the viewer to focus on the thing you want them to focus on.

If this sounds like a lot of work, it usually is. Giving successful presentations is difficult. But if you're not willing to put in the effort, then you're wasting your audience's time. And, you'll be leaving lots of meetings frustrated that your audience didn't adopt your desired point of view. But, if you change your perspective and realize that presentations have to be entertaining first and informative second, and you're willing to put in a bit of effort, you can be more persuasive and your presentations will affect the changes you want to make happen (like raising hundreds of millions of dollars for your startup).

If I had to boil down my advice on fundraising into three strategic principles, they would be as follows. First, it's best to raise money when you hit some type of inflection point based on some objective criterion that provides validation. Second, you should make sure you're building relationships with potential investors long before you need to raise money. Third, you should only raise money from investors who are excited about your vision and motivated to help you realize it.

One of the reasons strategic principles are helpful is that they highlight the things you should not do. For example, you should not try to raise money just because you need money; that violates the first strategic principle that says you should raise money when you meet an objective criterion that helps to validate part of your hypotheses for investors. When I raised my first pre-seed round, I had written a software library for machine learning that I could use as a prototype. Then, I raised our seed round after publishing a peer reviewed paper about a new type of neural network we had invented, and its application to forecasting the progression of Alzheimer's disease. These types of things give early investors reasons to believe you're not full of shit. In addition, I often talk to many founders who are just getting ready to talk to potential investors a few months before they'll need capital. No! This violates the second principle. You should always be talking to investors, grabbing coffee, and building relationships. You want to make sure the people you're taking money from are a good fit for you and your startup, and it will take time to get to know people. And, lastly, don't take money from investors who aren't a good fit for your company! If you don't like them, or if their priorities seem misplaced, don't accept the term sheet. It's not worth it.

Let's break down the fundraising process into a few more detailed steps.

1. Start Early: Begin meeting with VCs *at least* a year before you need to raise funds. These initial meetings are not for pitching but for relationship building. Do not bring a deck! Maybe meet over coffee or drinks if you can. Be super clear that you aren't raising money right now.

2. Build Relationships: Use these early meetings to gauge which investors are a good fit. Do you like them personally? Do they understand your business? Sort them into three tiers: best, mid, and worst fits for your company. Maintain regular contact with your top-tier investors, providing updates on your business, both good and bad.

3. Focus on Decision Makers: Make sure you're connecting with decision-makers in your top-tier firms. If not, ask your contact to bring in a partner. If they can't or won't, move them to the worst tier.

4. Engage Your Board Early: Discuss the raise with your board two quarters ahead of time. Agree on what the objective criterion is you'll be using to argue that you've hit an inflection point. Get alignment on round size, target valuation, and investor profile. Share your tiered list of investors for backchannel insights or warm introductions.

5. Craft a Compelling Vision: Make your vision big. VCs want to know if your business can become huge. It's probably not

big enough! Think big! Develop three clear, compelling reasons why you can realize this vision. The bigger the round, the more evidence you'll need. Use these to create a non-confidential deck that tells a story—not detailed financials. Use an audience transformation roadmap or similar framework to make sure you can present investors with your huge vision and your three reasons to believe within a compelling narrative.

6. Prepare Two Decks: A non-confidential deck for initial meetings, focusing on your vision and story. A second, confidential deck with high-level financials, tailored to what VCs want to see.

7. Fundraise with a Partner: Ideally, have one other person join you in the fundraising process. If you're a business side CEO, bring your CTO. If you're a technical CEO, bring your CFO or COO. They should be comfortable presenting and aligned with your vision. If they aren't aligned with your vision, they shouldn't be in your executive team anyway.

8. Tee up the Fundraising Process: Reach out to top and mid-tier investors with your non-confidential deck. Tell them you are thinking about kicking off a raise soon. Set up meetings to present your vision from your non-confidential deck. Hold back financials and your confidential deck for the second meeting, ask them to sign an NDA in between.

9. Manage the Process: Prepare your data room with the help of your law firm, ready roughly a week after your second meetings. Get around five potential leads into the data room simultaneously, ideally two from your top tier.

10. Keep Up the Momentum: Don't let investors linger; set clear decision deadlines. Be super helpful and responsive during this period, answer any of their questions clearly, concisely, and quickly. Aim for at least three partnership pitches. Make your presentation high-energy, thoughtful, and story-driven. Be authentic, nobody likes a bullshitter.

11. Don't Stop After a Term Sheet: Continue pitching to potential lead investors even after receiving a term sheet, but before you sign it. You can tell other investors that you've received a term sheet, but do not share any of the proposed terms or the identity of the lead investor with other investors. Term sheets are typically confidential. Many investors aim to follow-on in rounds led by others by writing smaller checks, and you should discuss these investors with your lead because they'll have opinions about who they like working with too.

12. Check References: Always check references on your lead investor, particularly if they are joining your board of directors. Make sure to talk to founders who are on boards with them. Treat these reference checks just as seriously as you would for an executive at your company. A bad board member is difficult to get rid of.

13. Close the Round: Term sheets have expiration dates; but they're fake -- don't let investors pressure you into signing at a specific time. As long as you're negotiating in good faith they will adjust the date. After you sign the term sheet, closing the actual will involve a month or so of detailed legal work—your investor's counsel needs those billable hours!—try not to lose your mind during it. Don't celebrate until the wires hit your

bank account; it's bad, but rounds can fall apart on the finish line sometimes.

14. Maintain Relationships Post-Raise: Fundraising never ever ever stops. Reach out to new investors a month after closing to keep relationships strong for future rounds. Go back to meeting over coffee or drinks, when possible, and catch up with each potential investor every few months.

15. Long-Term Perspective: Remember, you're not just raising money—you're recruiting a business partner who's likely to join your board in some capacity. Strong relationships with investors are key to long-term success, especially future fundraising rounds.

15. Chairman of the bored.

Yes, I know it's spelled "board of directors". But if you don't figure out how to communicate with your board members effectively, your board meetings will be boring and useless at best, and frustrating and exhausting at worst. You'll be chairman of the bored rather than chairman of the board. [1]

Most first time founders have difficulty working with their boards of directors. I sure did. This usually happens for three reasons. First, there is a power dynamic. Technically, the board of directors is the CEOs boss. You have to learn to ignore that, and good board members don't usually think of it that way. Second, your board of directors will know less about your business than you think they should. In fact, they will probably know less about business in general than you think they should. Don't succumb to the illusion that they know more than you, they do not. Third, you should not try to dive into

---

1. Credit for this joke goes to Norm MacDonald.

any details with your board of directors. A board should operate at a strategic level, but many first time founders struggle to keep out of the weeds.

There is also a fourth reason, which is you can have a bad board member. Only a few board members are actually helpful to early stage companies. Most board members are neutral. But, it's not that uncommon to end up with a really bad board member who adds negative value, who harms the company with their poor attitude and idiotic advice; it can even get to the point where it seems like they are actively trying to sabotage your company. Usually, the bad board members are venture capitalists. Some famous venture capitalists even have reputations for being terrible board members, so make sure to check references. Unfortunately, it's really difficult to get rid of a bad board member once they are on your board. The venture capital firm usually has the right to a board seat written into the company's by laws. Your only defense against this is to choose your investors wisely.

I think that board members should primarily care about the following things.

- What is the CEOs vision?
- What are the strategic principles the company must follow to achieve that vision?
- What are the cultural principles by which the company expects employees to behave?
- Has the executive team changed any of the above recently? Do they need to?
- Are there areas of dissonance where the company isn't living up to its stated principles?

- What is the most important thing for the company right now?
- What are the (up to 3) questions the CEO wants help or input from the board on?
- What is the runway? When would the company next need to raise money?

That's pretty much all I would want to know as a board member. And, that's the level at which you should target communications with your board.

You'll typically want to meet with your board once per quarter. This is usually a meeting that lasts roughly three hours. It's preferable to hold this meeting in the morning and to provide plenty of coffee. You should also invite board members to dinner the night before the board meeting. You should also have periodic one-on-one meetings with board members outside of formal meetings. Never surprise your board members in a board meeting! Use these one-on-ones to give them a heads up about any important issues before you raise them in a board meeting. I also think you should have frequent, informal communications with your board members. Not just about stuff related to your company, but general stuff you'd discuss with colleagues. Build the relationships. Chat over text or messenger apps. Meet for coffee or drinks. Etc.

As you prepare for a board meeting, remember that you will be spending roughly 10 hours per day on your company, but your board members will only be spending around 10 hours per quarter on it. It's not their fault they don't know what's going on, they aren't spending the same amount of time on it as you are. Your venture capital board members will probably be on many other boards too. So, you need to provide them with lots of context at every meeting. Do not assume that they remember what happened at the previous meeting, or that they know many details about your startup.

I think that the pre-read for a board meeting should be provided as a written memo, not as a slide deck, for reasons I explained earlier. You'll probably have some board members who complain about having to read the memo, but ignore their complaints. This memo should answer every one of the questions above, and it should have appendices that go into more details about important issues such as your financial statements, sales pipeline, and key performance indicators. You can provide the appendices in slide format as a compromise if you wish. Send these to the board approximately one week ahead of time, and then send a reminder the day before the board meeting. Remind them again at dinner the night before the meeting.

You should start every board meeting with a presentation about what your company does. This should take about 30 minutes, including some time for questions. And, yes, you should use a slide deck for this part of the meeting. Make sure this presentation describes your vision and what you're working on today. It should be similar to the style of presentation you'd give to venture capitalists with your non-confidential deck. This reminds your board of your vision and brings it top of mind, gives them context for the upcoming meeting, lets you set the tone, and gives you practice presenting to investors. Use the last 5 minutes of your presentation to talk about what you think the most important thing is for your company right now. This is what the most important thing is right now, and here's why. That's it. Keep all of your board meeting presentations simple and to the point.

Next, have a couple of other people from your company present to the board on some interesting topics. For example, you might have your CTO give them an overview of your recent technological developments. Or, you could have your VP of Product give them a demo of some upcoming features. Or, you could have your VP of Sales walk them through your sales pipeline. Make sure you coach your leadership team to keep these presentations high level, and to provide lots of context to your board members.

That should conclude the first half of your meeting. Give everyone a few minutes to take a short bio break and refill their coffee. Then, bring the board members and your legal counsel back for the second half of the meeting. Start the second half of the meeting by voting on any resolutions. These often include grants of stock options to new employees, and approval of the minutes from the previous board meeting. This should only take a few minutes. Make sure you always list both the total shares and the percentage of any option grants, and describe what the option pool is before and after the grants, to make that discussion go smoothly. Investors don't like it when you run out of options in your option pool because increasing it involves issuing new shares, which causes dilution. After you've voted, move on to discuss the questions you asked the board for input on in your memo. This should kick off an hour or so of strategic discussion. This is your opportunity to hear from your board members, not the other way around, so all you should be doing is directing the conversation and keeping it on track. Typically, your board members will ask you to step out for a few minutes at the end of the meeting, so that they can discuss your performance as CEO.

This approach aims to keep the board weighing in on the topics that you think are important. Your pre-read includes all the context and details, sets up what you think the top priority is right now, and directs the conversation towards a small number of topics you want the board to help with. Even though you asked them for help, you don't have to take their advice. Even if they yell at you about not listening, you don't have to take their advice. Treat your board members as advisers who can provide a fresh set of eyes about important issues, but who don't have all of the details necessary to make fully informed decisions. I don't believe that a board should ever overrule a CEO. If it comes to that point, then the board should grow a spine and replace the CEO. Therefore, whatever you do, don't let your board treat you like shit. Just keep chugging away at your vision with relentless intensity, listening to their advice but only acting on it when you think it makes sense. If they don't fire you after the meeting, then you still have their support.

Part Three
Building

Oh, so hot, no time to take a rest, yeah
Act tough, ain't room for second best
Real strong, got me some security
Hey, I'm a big smash, I'm goin' for infinity, yeah
If you think I'll sit around as the world goes by
You're thinkin' like a fool 'cause it's a case of do or die
Out there is a fortune waiting to be had
If you think I'll let you go, you're mad
You've got another thing comin'
You've got another thing comin'
You've got another thing comin'

Judas Priest

16. Principles are more important than plans.

What do you think about the following strategy for playing a game of chess as white? White makes the first move, so I'll open the game by moving a pawn from e2 to e4. Then, for my second move, I'll move a knight from g1 to f3. And, for my third move, I'll move a bishop from f1 to c4. Etc. If you're very familiar with chess (which I'm not, I had to look up this opening sequence) then you may recognize the first couple moves, but answering my question doesn't require much familiarity with chess at all. You don't even need to picture a chess board. If you know that there are two players, white and black, who take turns moving their pieces on a chessboard with the goal of capturing the other side's king, that's good enough. Because, in fact, this was a trick question. This is not a fucking strategy! It's a plan. A list of moves to be made in sequence, and not a very good one either because it doesn't adjust to the actions of the opponent. How could a chess player possibly say what moves they'll be making 3 or more steps ahead without knowing what moves their opponent is going to make?

In complex, open-ended, adaptive environments like a game of chess or building a startup (and, I guarantee you that building your startup will be much more complicated than a game of chess) it's not usually possible to reliably plan more than one or two steps ahead. To quote the great philosopher Harry Potter, "Hermione, when have any of our plans ever actually worked? We plan, we get there, all hell breaks loose." Nevertheless, most people want to waste time and energy creating a complicated plan. They will tell you that you need a business plan, an annual plan, a quarterly plan, etc. You'll even need a plan for planning! People afflicted by manageritis are especially fond of plans. Even worse, some people seem to be incapable of operating without such a plan, they cannot handle the ambiguity or uncertainty, and will freeze like a deer in the headlights without one. But, you cannot escape uncertainty because it's an inherent part of building a startup—actually, uncertainty is the defining feature of what it means to build a startup. As Jason Fried says, "a plan is just a guess you write down". [1] Don't spend much time worrying about writing down various guesses about what will happen in the future, and just get to work creating the future you want.

Unfortunately, many people in business seem to have confused the word 'strategy' for the word 'plan'. They will say you need to come up with an 'annual strategy' but what they are really asking for is an annual plan. They use oxymoronic terms like 'strategic planning'. So, let me set the record straight. A strategy and a plan are very different things. And, while I don't believe that it's a good idea to spend much time planning, I

---

1. https://signalvnoise.com/svn3/planning-is-guessing/

think it's absolutely necessary to create a strategy and to revisit it frequently.

Writing in Harvard Business Review, Michael Watkins states that "[a] business strategy is a set of guiding principles that, when communicated and adopted in the organization, generates a desired pattern of decision making." [2] Please read that definition again. A strategy is a set of guiding principles, it is not a plan.

Let's go back to the chess example and take a look at a simple strategy defined by three principles.

1. Develop your pieces quickly: Aim to mobilize your key pieces early in the game to maximize their influence and prepare for both attack and defense.
2. Control the center: Aim to dominate the center of the board to gain space and create stronger positions for your pieces.
3. Activity over material advantage: Aim to prioritize the effectiveness and positioning of your pieces over simply accumulating more pieces, as active pieces can often outweigh material gains.

None of these principles state which specific moves to make, but they provide guidelines to help a player judge what to do next at any point in the game. For example, in order to control the center, it may be a good idea to start with a move like pawn e2 to e4 that places one of your pieces in the center of the board. Then, in order to develop your pieces quickly, it may be

---

2. https://hbr.org/2007/09/demystifying-strategy-the-what

a good idea to follow that up by moving knight g1 to f3 so that you have an active knight. The strategy also provides a player with guidelines on things they shouldn't do. For example, an opening move of pawn a2 to a3 at the edge of the board would not fit with this strategy because it's not helping to control the center. Thus, the principles determine the plan, not the other way around. A player guided by strategic principles can quickly adjust their tactics, or change their plan, in response to moves by the other player.

To come up with a business strategy, start from your vision and work backwards to come up with a set of 3-5 core principles. The idea is, if you generally follow these principles, then you'll likely be successful in achieving your vision. These principles should be clear, concise, and actionable. For example, if someone at your company is thinking about what they should do to solve some problem, they should turn to your strategic principles to figure out what types of approaches they would or would not follow. Anyone at your company should be able to understand what they mean, and how they can apply them to their job.

Let's take a look at some example strategic principles for some well-known companies to get a better idea of what a business strategy looks like.

<u>Example Strategic Principles for Amazon</u>

1. Largest Selection: Amazon aims to offer an

unparalleled range of products to meet virtually any customer need.

2. Lowest Prices: By focusing on operational efficiency and economies of scale, Amazon strives to offer products at competitive prices.
3. Maximum Convenience: Amazon invests heavily in its logistics and fulfillment networks to provide quick and reliable delivery.

These strategic principles don't tell you what Amazon does, rather they tell you why Amazon does what they do. For example, why does Amazon primarily engage in internet commerce rather than opening up retail stores? Because the shelf space of a retail store is limited whereas the shelf space of a website is effectively infinite. Specializing in internet commerce is a tactic that allows them to offer the largest selection of products. Likewise, why would Amazon create a device like Alexa? Because it increases convenience.

<u>Example Strategic Principles for Apple</u>

1. Insanely Great User Experience: Apple creates insanely great products with minimalist designs that are intuitive and easy to use.
2. Integrated Ecosystem: Providing a seamless experience across all devices and services encourages customers to stay within the Apple ecosystem.
3. Premium Branding: Apple positions itself as a premium brand, offering high-quality, innovative products that justify higher price points.

These strategic principles are reflected in everything Apple does, from the clean lines of the iPhone case, to the integration of Macs, iPhones, iPads, and Apple Watches through the MacOS and iOS ecosystem, to the way products are presented in Apple retail stores like premium items rather than simply placed in boxes on shelves.

<u>Example Strategic Principles for Tesla</u>

1. Futuristic Designs: Accelerate the transition to sustainable energy by making cool products with futuristic designs.
2. Technologically Advanced Products: Delivering products that offer superior performance by pushing technological boundaries.
3. Direct-to-Consumer: Tesla sells directly to customers so that they can offer lower prices and enhance the buying experience to build strong customer relationships.

Think about some of the things Tesla has done recently, and try to figure out how they align with this strategy. The out of the box design of the Cybertruck. The push to build fully autonomous cars, buses, trucks, and robotaxis. The expansion into robotics with the development of the humanoid robot, Optimus. The development of lower price cars like the Model 3.

Let's do one more example. This time, however, let's try to come up with some strategic principles for a hypothetical company with the following vision:

<u>Example Strategic Principles for A Hypothetical New Company</u>

Vision: We will develop energy storage technology so powerful and efficient that it will decouple human civilization from traditional power grids, enabling a sustainable future where every home, vehicle, and city can generate, store, and distribute their own clean energy, revolutionizing global energy independence.

1. Maximum Energy Efficiency: Continuously develop new technologies to achieve the highest energy efficiency possible, limited only by the laws of physics.
2. High Quality at Affordable Prices: Provide top-quality energy storage products at prices that make them accessible to a wide range of customers.
3. Scalable and Modular Solutions: Design flexible systems that can be easily scaled and adapted for use anywhere, from individual homes to entire cities.

We develop innovative, energy-efficient, and sustainable technologies to provide high-quality, user-friendly energy solutions at affordable prices. By offering scalable and modular systems that meet diverse needs—from individual homes to entire cities—we empower customers worldwide, support widespread adoption, and advance global energy independence while maintaining environmental responsibility.

Once you have articulated your strategic principles, you use them as a guide to come up with your top priorities. Every employee at your company needs to be able to describe your vision, your cultural principles, and your strategic principles. Repeat them often. Have your co-founders repeat them often. Have your leadership team repeat them often. Print them out on posters and plaster them on the walls of your office. I guarantee you that someone will tell you that you aren't spending enough time planning, that although they understand the strategy they don't know how to translate it to concrete actions. They may not be a good fit for an early stage startup. At the early stage, it is a complete waste of time for you to come up with a plan. You need a vision, a strategy, and your top priorities. Then you need to get to work. Plans are not useful until much later, when you need to coordinate activities across a large number of employees or communicate with many external parties like growth stage or public market investors. Even then, the most well thought out plan will still amount to nothing more than a guess.

17. Prioritize ruthlessly

"What is your top priority right now?" I would ask. "Well, I'm working on many things right now and all of them are important," would come the inevitable reply. "Okay," I would say, "Please take out a piece of paper and write them down for me, in order from most to least important." Then I would wait, perhaps adding the prompt, "Yes, I'm serious," if my colleague looked particularly bewildered. After they finished writing down the things they were working on—which could sometimes take 5 to 10 minutes—I would say, "Thank you. Now, what's the first item?" In an ordered list, there is always one single item at the top. During the nearly 8 years that I was a first time CEO, I would estimate that I had a conversation like this once per week, on average. I never got the impression that the person on the other side of the conversation enjoyed it, in fact they were usually rather annoyed with me, but making fun conversation isn't a CEOs most important job, creating focus is.

According to Rebecca Homkes, author of "Survive, Reset, Thrive: Leading Breakthrough Growth Strategy in Volatile Times," Steve Jobs would take his top 100 employees on a retreat each year. Notice that I did not say Apple's 100 highest ranking employees according to the org chart, I said Steve's top 100 employees; the people he considered to be part of the "A team" at Apple. That's an important lesson, but it's an aside from my main point. Anyway, at the retreat the Apple "A team" would talk about the vision, strategic principles, and industry trends that could act as headwinds or tailwinds over the next year. Then, at the end of the session he would have the team write down a list of the ten most important things they thought Apple should do next. Once the team was done debating their ideas, and had written down the ten most important things to do next as an ordered list, Steve would walk up to the front of the room and cross out the last seven. "We can only do three," he would say.

At PayPal, Peter Theil reportedly instituted a management style based on "extreme focus" in which every employee was expected to focus on a single task—just the task with the current maximum priority. According to Keith Rabois, Peter created this culture at PayPal by refusing to discuss anything with an employee other than their currently assigned top priority.[1] In addition, annual employee evaluations didn't ask employees to list all of the things they did during the year or to identify something like their top three accomplishments, instead, employees were asked to identify their single most

---

1. https://www.quora.com/PayPal-product/What-strong-beliefs-on-culture-for-entrepreneurialism-did-Peter-Max-and-David-have-at-PayPal/answer/Keith-Rabois

valuable contribution to the company that year. Just. One. Single. Thing.

In his book, "Amp it up", the former CEO of ServiceNow and Snowflake, Frank Slootman, says that the best leaders maintain a singular focus. "'Priority' should ideally be used as a singular word. The moment you have many priorities, you actually have none," he says. To maintain a singular focus, he recommends stop trying to execute many tasks in parallel and to instead focus on executing tasks sequentially (more on this below), and that leaders constantly re-rank their objectives and to focus all of their effort on the one at the top.

I'm sure I could continue to find more examples of famous business leaders expressing the same idea—have a ruthless, extreme, singular focus on the most important thing. Unfortunately, no matter how many times you read it, keeping that singular focus is one of the hardest parts of running a startup.

The will to force extreme prioritization is a common trait of the best CEOs and leaders. Make no mistake; ruthless prioritization isn't a principle that you can easily implement. It takes discipline and willpower. Most people find this level of prioritization unnatural and uncomfortable. Ruthless prioritization is an extreme, continuous form of decision making. Anyone who is even a little bit indecisive will struggle with this level of prioritization. As with most things in life, there are both good and bad reasons for the resistance many employees express when it comes time to prioritize.

We can examine some of the advantages and disadvantages of prioritization by making an analogy to parallel and sequential processing in computer science. Early computers had a single processing core that would perform one instruction at a time. Thus, programs were executed sequentially. Open the file, then read the first word, then read the second word, and so on. Modern computers contain multi-core central processing units (CPUs) in addition to graphical processing units (GPUs) that may contain hundreds or even thousands of processing cores. A program can break a computation up into smaller chunks, and send these chunks out to be processed by different cores at the same time—in parallel—then the results of each processed chunk are collected and combined to get the complete result. If your computer has N processing cores, then a computation that is easy to parallelize could be up to N times faster with this setup. That is, a dual core computer could be up to twice as fast as a single core computer, at least in principle.

Unfortunately, not all computations are easy to parallelize. In fact, some computations cannot be parallelized at all and have to be performed sequentially instead, one thing at a time. Even for computations that can be parallelized, parallelization usually comes with a cost that prevents one from realizing all of the potential gains. Programs that perform computations in parallel require additional time to start and terminate each thread, and incur communication costs if any information needs to be shared between threads. In addition, the programmer who is designing an algorithm to run in parallel needs to worry about synchronizing activities across the threads, which can result in errors due to a race condition when two threads try to modify something in shared memory at the same time. If thread 1 completes before thread 2, then the program executes instruction 1 before instruction 2. But, if thread 2 completes before thread 1, then the program executes instruction 2 before instruction 1. That's fine in some programs if the order of the instructions doesn't matter, but what if it does? As a result, writing programs that can run in parallel efficiently is much more difficult than writing simple sequential programs, it takes longer to write the first version of the program, longer to optimize it, and requires more effort to debug and maintain.

Trying to complete multiple tasks at the same time in an organization is analogous to a program that executes a computation in parallel. And, a leader who asks (or allows) their organization to take on too many tasks at the same time will encounter analogous costs. There is a cost to starting up a team to take on a new project. There is a large communication overhead, especially if these teams need to share information, or if there are dependencies across the projects. There are synchronization problems if one team completes their project well ahead of another, especially if the faster team is blocked while waiting on the output from the slower team. Creating an organization that can efficiently perform many tasks in parallel is much more complex than creating an organization to execute a few high priority items sequentially. Your organization will need more managers (each of whom will command a high salary), your employees will have to spend more time in meetings (which incurs an opportunity cost), and teams will have more disagreements and miscommunications (which will be frustrating and draining). People afflicted by manageritis resist prioritization because it reduces the need for managers and their power in the organization, but that's why you should love prioritization.

Obviously, some tasks can be completed in parallel by different teams in your company. These are tasks that don't have obvious dependencies, and require little or no communication between teams. Your finance team can close the books from your last quarter, while your engineers simultaneously work to update your front end. These tasks are embarrassingly parallel. No extra effort is needed to split the problem into smaller chunks that can be executed simultaneously. It should be pretty obvious when tasks like this have basically zero dependencies.

The defining problems at startups are not easily parallelizable. They are inherently sequential. That's because startups are defined by uncertainty. The tasks of building a startup, launching a product, or creating a new technology are types of search problems. You do not actually know the best way to solve the problem, instead you are searching for a good solution through a process of trial and error. While there are search algorithms that operate in parallel, they are generally wasteful because they tend to spend a lot of effort looking in the wrong place. In the case of a computer algorithm, this means wasting energy; in the case of a company, it means wasting money. In some rare cases, it can be worth throwing lots of money at a problem to enable a parallel search, but I think that first time entrepreneurs should not have the hubris to try that strategy. Instead, I think entrepreneurs should approach these search problems like a Metropolis algorithm.

The Metropolis algorithm was invented in physics as a way to search for low energy configurations of a system. First, you make an initial guess and evaluate its energy. Then, you make a small change to that guess to create a new configuration. Next, you evaluate the energy of the new potential configuration. If the energy of the new configuration is lower than the energy of your previous configuration, then you update your guess to the new configuration. Otherwise, you go back to your previous configuration and try a different way to modify it.

Imagine that you're building a web application with multiple pages. To start, you make a guess by creating a prototype or minimum viable product. Then, you get some customers to evaluate your initial guess. Based on this feedback, you formulate a hypothesis you could make the largest improvement in your product by redesigning one particular element. So, you focus on that top priority, modify it, and then go back to your customers so they can reevaluate your updated product. If your hypothesis was correct and they do, in fact, think the product is improved, then you accept your new design and come up with a new hypothesis about the next feature worth adding or updating. But, it's possible that customers don't like your new design as much as your old design, in which case you should abandon the new design for the previous version, and then reformulate your hypothesis about how to improve the original design. This is essentially a Metropolis algorithm.

You can apply this approach as a tool for discovering solutions to nearly any problem. It is sequential and iterative. At each step, you have a current solution (which is the best solution you've found so far) and a new proposed solution (which you think could be better). In the Metropolis algorithm, it's important not to change too many things between proposals. That is, your new proposed solution should be similar to your current solution, preferably with a single additional feature or update. If you try to change too many things between proposed solutions, you'll end up rejecting most of your proposals and you will make very slow progress. One could make more complicated analogies, but I think you get the idea.

The state of the universe is one of constantly increasing entropy. It is easier to add items to your to-do list, than to cross things off. Therefore, your to-do list will continue to grow unless you make an extra effort to keep it under control. Work is required to decrease entropy.

Here is a concrete framework for ruthless prioritization.

Your company should have a single, high level, annual objective. To create this objective, get together with your team towards the end of the year for a three day long brainstorming session. In the early days, just bring your entire team. If you have more than a dozen people or so, then just bring the 10 people who you think are the best at strategic thinking. Spend the first day revisiting your mission, vision, strategic and cultural principles. Do you need to adjust your strategic principles? Are you living up to your cultural principles, or are you falling short? Next, spend the second day brainstorming a list of potential priorities. Come up with a list of the top ten things the team thinks your company should do in the next year, just like Steve Jobs would do with his team at Apple. On the third day, formulate a single, concrete objective for the year that would drive you to accomplish as many of the things on your top ten list as possible. To be clear, I'm suggesting that you be more extreme than Jobs, who allowed three priorities. You will only allow your team one single annual objective. This is the challenging part, coming up with a single objective that will serve as the North Star for your company over the next year. As an example, Frank Slootman describes creating a singular objective to focus on transforming "our rather industrial user experience to a consumer-grade service experience" at ServiceNow because accomplishing it would require them to evolve their entire engineering, product, and go-to-market practices.

Each team at your company should have a single, concrete quarterly objective. Towards the end of each quarter, you should have the leader of each team get together with their team members for a half-day long brainstorm. Each team will come up with a list of three potential priorities they could focus on over the next quarter. Next, gather all of your team leaders together for their own half-day brainstorm. Have them discuss the potential priorities their teams put together, placing a particular emphasis on noting any dependencies. Identify which priorities could be done in an embarrassingly parallel fashion, and which would require more cross-team communication. Finally, each team lead must formulate a single objective that will serve as the North Star for their team during the coming quarter.

Each person at your company should have a single, concrete objective that they are working on at any given time. At the beginning of the quarter, the members of each team should get together and review their team's singular quarterly objective, and they should each come up with a single thing that they need to get done right now. They will work on that single thing until it is done, they determine that it cannot be done (which will happen a lot at startups developing new technologies), or new information arises that requires a pivot in the team's priority. Once they finish their top priority, they should formulate a new top priority to work on in the same way. That is, they move from one top priority task to another, sequentially.

You can reinforce ruthless prioritization in your company by asking each employee to start each week by answering two simple questions: "What is your top priority this week?," and "What important task are you choosing to not do right now so that you can focus on your top priority?" You can pose these questions to a few randomly chosen employees at the start of the week, or ask all employees to send them to you via email or Slack similar to Jensen Huang at Nvidia. Spending a few minutes at the start of the week to get focused on their top priority will help all of your employees, and reading these messages will help you understand what everyone in your company is focused on.

Making a decision is always better than not making a decision. Setting a top priority is always better than setting too many priorities. But, what happens if you choose the wrong thing as your North Star? What happens if a project fails, or some new information comes to light? Simple. Just go back and change the objective. This is easy if an individual needs to change their objective, they just need to meet with the other members of the team and come up with the next thing they should focus on. It's a bit more complicated if a team needs to change their objective. In that case, the team leads should meet to agree on a new objective for that team, then the team lead should meet with their team members to formulate a new objective for each individual team member. It's a bit more complicated still if the company needs to adjust its annual objective, but that's fine. If you think that's necessary, then you simply need to gather your leadership together, discuss what's changed, and then reformulate your annual objective. Your team leads and individual contributors will follow that up by going back through the same process they did at the beginning of the quarter to formulate their singular objectives. You must always remain agile.

In summary, at any given time your company should have a single, top level annual objective. Each team should have a single, concrete quarterly objective. And each individual should have a single, top priority task they are working on at the moment. Individuals move from one task to another sequentially, so that they're always focusing on a single task of maximum priority.

18. You must decide!

Indecision is an anchor that will slowly drag your company to the bottom of the sea. And second guessing a decision is an explosive that will blow your company right out of the water! The key to success in running a company is the ability to make difficult decisions quickly, and to stick with them long enough to see if they were right or wrong. This is especially true for you and anyone you select for your leadership team, but also applies to every single employee at your company.

Unfortunately, it's not easy to make difficult decisions. Nevertheless, you will have to make them all the time. A decision may be difficult because it comes attached to an emotion. Perhaps you know that one of your team members is performing poorly—poorly enough to justify moving them out of the company—but you like the person and don't want to hurt their feelings. Other times, a decision may be difficult because you're highly uncertain about the right course of action. You assign a 51% chance that option A is correct, and a

49% chance that option B is correct. Sometimes you will have to make key decisions based on little or no data because it would take too long or cost too much to collect the data needed to clarify the optimal choice. And sometimes a decision can be difficult even when there's a lot of data pointing in the right direction because the cost of choosing incorrectly is very high. You assign a 99% chance that option A is correct and only a 1% chance that option B is correct, but if you choose A instead of B and you're wrong your company will go out of business.

You must accept the following five principles of decision making. The first principle is simply that someone must decide. Even if the decision is difficult, someone has to make it. If someone does not make the decision, then nobody will know what to do. Not making the decision is the worst course of action. Although this seems obvious, most people hesitate when faced with difficult decisions in the hopes that the decision will be made for them, either by someone else or because some new data will magically appear and rule out the incorrect path. The second principle is that you—the founder and CEO —should be the one to make the most difficult decisions. Whoever makes the most difficult decisions is the person in charge. It doesn't matter if you have the title of CEO, if you let others around you make the most difficult decisions, or if you insist on reaching consensus, then they are the ones who are actually in charge. The third principle is that you cannot and should not make all of the decisions. If someone approaches you to ask you to make a decision, you should first figure out if it is a sufficiently difficult decision that it actually requires your attention. If it is not sufficiently difficult, then you should tell them that they need to make the call themselves. If they are unable to make the call themselves, then they are not able to be a leader at your company. The fourth principle is that you must try to keep your emotions in check when you are making key decisions. The most difficult emotion to check when faced with a difficult decision is fear. Everyone would feel fear if faced with a difficult decision that could destroy their company if they make the wrong move. Nevertheless, the first and second principles state that you must decide anyway, so you must learn to accept this fear and be decisive. Finally, the fifth principle is that you must not second guess your decision once you have made it. Once you choose that path to take, you must put any fears you previously had aside. Run down that path with the intention to blast through any obstacle you encounter along the way. Damn the torpedoes! Full steam ahead!

Note that refusing to second guess a key decision doesn't mean that you will never change your mind. Instead, it means that you should not hedge your bets. Once you make a decision, you and the rest of your team need to go all in on it and try like hell to make it work. Then, you need to give it enough time to see results. In some cases, it might only take a month to collect enough data to know if you've made the right call. In other cases, it could take a year or more. Once you've seen it through, if the data point in another direction, then you can change your mind.

Jeff Bezos popularized a useful framework for classifying different types of decisions. [1] Although some decisions are one way doors, most decisions are two way doors. A one way door

---

1. https://aws.amazon.com/executive-insights/content/how-amazon-defines-and-operationalizes-a-day-1-culture/

is a decision that cannot be undone; or, at least, one that is difficult to undo. For example, once you decide to open source a piece of software you cannot de-open source it. From that point on, that piece of code will be in the public domain. A two way door is a decision that is relatively easy to undo. You walk through it and, if you don't like what you find on the other side, you can simply turn around and come back. For example, suppose you decide that black should be the primary color of your new website. But, you soon start hearing feedback from customers that your new branding isn't resonating with them. A few months go by and the tide isn't turning, so you simply go back and change the primary color of your website to white. You ran an experiment and it didn't work out. No big deal.

Two way doors should not be treated as difficult decisions because you can always reverse course if necessary. Therefore, the first thing that you, or anyone else on your team, should do when faced with a decision is to classify it as a one way door or a two way door. You should make sure to explain the concept of one way and two way doors to all of your employees on their first day. You should go through some examples to make sure they understand the difference. Then, you should explain that you expect them to make two way door decisions themselves, rather than bringing such decisions to management. My preferred approach to making a decision when faced with a two way door is to just go with my gut, my first instinct. My personality lends itself to intuition, and I've now honed my intuition through many years of experience. Other people may prefer to apply some type of framework to help them make the decision, and that's okay as long as they don't take too long deliberating. Two way doors aren't worth long periods of deliberation. Usually, making a simple list of pros and cons will do. If you ingrain this message into all of your employees from the beginning and, of course, hire high agency people to begin with, then most of the two way door decisions will be made by others in your organization. Not all of them, however, because you will still face some two way doors yourself while working on projects within your area of expertise. If anyone comes to you for help making a two way door decision, don't make it for them. Instead, repeat your message from your onboarding about one way doors and two way doors, suggest that they make a list of pros and cons, and force the issue by giving them a deadline by which they need to make the call.

If you do a good job hiring high agency employees and training them on the difference between one way and two way doors, then most of the decisions you'll have to make (outside of the projects you take on in your area of expertise) will be one way doors. Even still, not all one way doors are difficult decisions. If you face a one way door, and the consequences of making an incorrect decision are negligible, then it doesn't really matter that it's irreversible. You'll only pay a small cost for being wrong. For example, suppose you want to purchase a product that cannot be returned. If the product costs $1, then it doesn't really matter. The worst case scenario is that you don't like the product, but you've only lost $1. No big deal. Such a decision would be much more difficult if the product was really expensive, like if it cost $1M. Therefore, the second thing you should do when faced with a decision is try to estimate the magnitude of the consequence of being wrong. If the consequences of being wrong are negligible, then I suggest having someone else at your company make the call.

By applying this framework, only the most difficult decisions will filter up to you. You will be left looking at one way doors, in which there are very serious consequences for making the wrong choice. It is your job as founder and CEO to make these decisions. You should absolutely take some time to deliberate on these decisions. You should talk to people throughout your company to gather the facts. You may also want to talk to external experts. You should listen to people within your organization debate the issue. In fact, it can be useful to organize a debate within your leadership team in which you assign teams to represent each choice in a debate. On the other hand, it's also helpful to let people voice their opinions (as opposed to presenting a prepared argument) because intuition can be a powerful tool for decision making. You should avoid giving your opinion or letting anyone know which way you're leaning while you are engaged in your fact finding mission or during these debates. Personally, I find this difficult to do because I have a poor quality filter between my brain and my mouth. One thing that helps is to timebox the fact finding and debating activities so that you pre-specify on which date you'll be making the decision. For example, if you say that you'll communicate your decision to the team on Friday, when someone on Wednesday inevitably asks you which way you're leaning you can simply reply that you'll let them know your decision on Friday. They will probably be annoyed with you, but that's part of being the boss.

You should always write a one page memo to communicate what decision you've made and the reason you've made it. You should share this memo with your entire company, not just your leadership team, as long as there's no legal reason not to or a particularly sensitive issue involved. In fact, it's useful to create an easy to find store of these memos to catalog all of your key decisions for your whole company. Once you've made this decision, you and your entire organization must not hesitate to see it through. It doesn't matter if people on your team disagree with your decision. They must all put that aside and commit to running full steam ahead immediately. If they will not do that, then you must remove them from your team immediately. Second guessing key decisions is a form of simple sabotage. This goes for you too. Even if you were racked by fear during your deliberations, lying awake at night worried about the consequences of making the wrong move, you must destroy those fears once you have made the call. You must charge forward. No, you must lead the charge! Your team must see you move without hesitation and with conviction in your chosen direction. Then, they will follow you into battle.

19. The rule of four

There's an old joke in software engineering that goes something like this: if one engineer can finish a project in one month, then six engineers can finish the project in six months!

When the steps in a computation can be performed in an embarrassingly parallel fashion, the rate at which the computation can be completed increases roughly linearly with the number of computational cores. Two cores will be twice as fast as one core. Three cores will be three times as fast. Etc. Unfortunately, few tasks are easily parallelizable. Communication overhead means that there are diminishing returns to using more cores for the computation. In practice, two cores is only 1.5 times as fast as one core. And three cores is only two times as fast as one core. Etc. The same is true in organizations, except the scaling is much worse. In fact, the surest way to ensure the failure of a project is to keep putting more people on it.

Ideally, a single project should be assigned to a single team. If a project is too large for a single team to handle on its own in the time allotted, then the project should be split up into chunks to be executed in parallel by additional teams. This will create overhead of course, but if that's the only way to complete the project before the deadline then you'll have to pay that cost.

Each team needs to have an individual designated as the team leader. The team leader's job is to make sure that the team remains focused on its singular objective, that each team member remains focused on one task at a time, that tasks are completed sequentially and that appropriate adjustments are made along the way. The people on the team do not need to report to the team leader as they would in a traditional management structure. In fact, the person who is designated as team leader could even change from time-to-time depending on what project the team is taking on. Hierarchy is not important. Accountability and focus are important. Each team needs an individual leader to make sure that the team maintains focus, and to make sure there is a single individual who is accountable for the team's performance on that project. Shared ownership is no ownership.

For small projects, it's possible to have a team of one. The team leader is simply responsible for themselves. Larger projects will require more people; though, the team leader should always be a player/coach. But how many more people? The answer is a maximum of three other people.

As a general rule of thumb (which I typically credit to my co-founder Aaron Smith), the productivity of a team begins to decrease when it grows beyond four people. That is, a team of four people may (or may not) be more productive than a team of three people. But, a team of five people is always less productive than a team of four people! Therefore, you should always try to minimize the number of people on any given team.

Minimizing the number of people on a team is beneficial because it increases the speed of decision making, decreases communication overhead, and forces prioritization. The first two things are pretty obvious; if there are fewer cooks in the kitchen, then team members will find it easier to communicate and stay in alignment. But, people often forget about the latter benefit—forcing prioritization—even though it is the most important. A team with too many people on it will fall prey to Parkinson's law: the work will expand to fill the time of the team members. People don't like to sit around twiddling their thumbs. As a result, if you put too many people on a project they will start to come up with new tasks to do, even if these tasks are low priority and are likely to result in little to no impact. This is an unavoidable consequence of making teams too big. The only way to avoid it is to keep teams small. Small teams have limited bandwidth, which forces them to focus solely on the highest priority items.

People who are afflicted by manageritis often want to hire more people to avoid making difficult prioritization decisions. They will tell you that their small team cannot possibly make progress on its assigned project, and they will justify this stance by coming to you with a long list of priorities—a list with ten or more items on it, for example. When this happens, and it will happen, force them to choose a single item on their list for their team to focus on and cross out everything else. If they refuse, then you need to move them out of your company immediately.

Teams do not need to reflect an explicit hierarchy like they do in traditional organizations. In fact, they usually shouldn't. I do not believe that one should regard the team as the fundamental unit of an organization. Instead, a company is a collection of individuals who organize into teams in order to complete projects. The projects are the fundamental element that dictate how the teams should be organized, not the other way around.

Traditional organizations look like bloated pieces of legacy software. There are many pre-defined modules and classes with specific functionality. In order to write a program, the programmer needs to figure out how to mold the computation they want to perform into something that can be represented by these modules and classes. If they are finding it too difficult to mold their problem in this way because the existing framework is too restrictive, then they have to refactor the library by shuffling around various modules and classes until the library is easier to work with. If you've been at pretty much any company before, you'll recognize this exact pattern occurring frequently as company "reorganizations".

Rather than thinking of a program in terms of objects, one can alternatively break a program down into smaller jobs to be done (i.e., functions). Likewise, I believe that companies should work backwards from their objectives. Figure out what projects you need to complete in order to meet your objective.

Then, stand up a team around each one of these projects. Assign one person as the team lead, and assign as few additional team members as necessary (up to a maximum of four) in order to complete the project in the desired timeframe. Thus, I believe that team membership is fluid because it is adapting to do the jobs that need to be done when they need to be done.

This is actually a pretty radical point of view. Most employees are used to the hierarchy of a traditional organization. In fact, many have come to depend upon it. They judge their career progression by where they sit within this hierarchy, rather than by the impact they have delivered to the organization. This is, of course, terrible. A burgeoning symptom of manageritis. However, that doesn't mean I support completely flat organizations. There are some well-known companies that have experimented with completely flat organizations and, although I've never worked at one myself, I know people who have and they generally didn't have a good experience. With too little structure, a company devolves into a little kids hockey game in which every player flocks to the puck instead of playing a position. Rather uncharacteristically, I'm advocating for a middle ground. You should set up your company with a relatively small leadership team that sets the priorities and organizes people into teams based on the projects that need to get done. You're aiming to keep the number of people in management roles to a minimum, but not at zero.

Speed is the most important characteristic that a startup needs in order to be successful. The best way to increase your pace is to focus on a small number of things, and to assign each of those things to a small team with a single individual as the team leader. This will help you to avoid some classic issues that I call "decelerators".

Decelerator 1: Lack of clear individual responsibility.

Every deliverable, and every decision, needs a single person who is responsible for it. Shared ownership is no ownership. Every decision should be documented with the name of the person who made it. Every requirement should be documented with the name of the person who wrote it. Not a group of people. Not two people. One person, who puts their name on it and owns it. This is one of Elon Musk's well-known principles for running companies.

Decelerator 2: Unclear goals and timelines.

The individual who owns the outcome for a project—i.e., the team leader—must commit to a clear goal and timeline and then hit it. The goal needs to be concrete and measurable so that there is no ambiguity about whether or not it was hit. The owner is responsible for making sure these are clear to all members of the team, to all the other team leaders in case there are dependencies, and they are responsible for asking for clarification from you or the other team leads if needed.

Decelerator 3: Consensus building.

Consensus feels safe because if everybody agreed then nobody can be singled out for being wrong. But if nobody can be singled out for being wrong, then there is no individual person responsible for the decision. Building consensus is shirking your individual responsibility. Of course you should get feedback, but when the time comes you need to make the call and put your name on it. And, everyone else on your team needs to commit to helping drive the best results possible now that the decision has been made. Anyone who will not make and honor that commitment is not a team player and should get off the team, and any team leader who frequently strives to reach consensus in decision making is unfit to lead.

Decelerator 4: Slow feedback cycles and poor communication.

The individual who owns the outcome for a project must be proactive about seeking feedback and communicating with the right people early and often. The right amount of communication will probably feel like overcommunication. People generally overestimate how much other people are paying attention to them, this is known as the spotlight effect. Everyone is paying less attention to you and your team than you think they are; generally, those people are busy worrying about their own shit. Therefore, you have to go the extra mile to make sure they know what they need to know about what you're doing. The team lead is also responsible for seeking clarifying feedback as needed; if you're the owner of a project and you're confused about something you should ask around and get clarity.

Decelerator 5: Pivoting too much.

Being nimble requires one to make quick course corrections as new information arises; it does not mean you should pivot around wildly and lose your sense of direction. Creating a fast moving ambitious startup requires courage to stay on course in some rough seas. You have to remain steadfast when it comes to your vision, but make quick and small adjustments to the details. Imagine that you are climbing a mountain, you should obviously walk around obstacles in your immediate path but it doesn't make sense to frequently switch the route you're taking to the summit.

Decelerator 6: Perfectionism.

Perfect is the enemy of good. Sometimes, actually pretty much all the time, you need to accept good enough. The team lead needs to know what "good enough" means for their project. If it's unclear to them, they are responsible for clarifying it. Sometimes it's possible to "fix things in post", in which case it's often better to ship the current version and fix it later. The people building something often do a surprisingly poor job predicting how others will respond to it; sometimes the builders think they've made something great only to find out their customers hate it, and sometimes the builders think they've made something shitty only to find out their customers love it. If you don't ship it, you'll never know.

Decelerator 7: Putting processes, tools, or activities over results.

Jeff Bezos said this best, "Good process serves you so you can serve customers. But if you're not watchful, the process can become the thing. This can happen very easily in large organizations. The process becomes the proxy for the result you want. You stop looking at outcomes and just make sure you're doing the process right. Gulp. It's not that rare to hear a junior leader defend a bad outcome with something like, "Well, we followed the process." A more experienced leader will use it as an opportunity to investigate and improve the process. The process is not the thing. It's always worth asking, do we own the process or does the process own us? In a Day 2 company, you might find it's the second." [1] It's generally difficult to get people to focus on results instead of processes, tools, or activities. Maybe someone has used a process successfully before. Maybe they like a particular tool and want others to use it too. Maybe they're more comfortable being held accountable to the activities they control, instead of results they can't fully control. But processes don't matter. Tools don't matter. Activities don't matter. Results matter. Period.

---

1. https://www.sec.gov/Archives/edgar/data/1018724/000119312517120198/ d373368dex991.htm

20. That word doesn't mean what you think it means

Entrepreneurs and investors in Silicon Valley are in love with the idea of disruption, but it often seems like few of them know what that word actually means. People frequently use the word disrupt as a synonym for revolutionize. Just say revolutionize if that's what you mean! Disruption refers to a particular strategy that a company can follow in order to revolutionize an industry, but there are other ways to revolutionize things. In any case, disruption is an extremely useful strategy. I suggest you figure out how to make it work for you.

Disruption refers to a strategy in which a company initially creates a product that targets a small niche of an existing or previously ignored market, and then steadily improves that product in order to expand into the rest of the market. [1] The concept was originally studied from the point of view of market incumbents, because incumbents often struggle to

---

1. The Innovator's Dilemma by Clayton Christensen

respond to disruptive innovations until it's too late. Just look at what's happened to Intel in the last few years after they missed the chance to lead the development of graphical processing units. Initially, the disruptive innovation looks like a niche product to the incumbent, so it's not worth their time and effort to worry about it. Often, incumbents look at disruptive innovations dismissively in the beginning. But, as the new product gets better it starts to eat into more of their market share. By the time they wake up and start to take the new innovation seriously, it's too late. Disruption is one of the primary causes of death for large corporations.

Disruptive innovations are often associated with a strategy in which a startup creates an initial product that targets low end users. The rise of the personal computer in the 1970s and 1980s is a famous example. When they were first introduced, personal computers were considered vastly inferior to large mainframe computers being used by big companies, but they became popular with hobbyists because they were much more affordable. Eventually, microprocessors improved so much that personal computers largely displaced mainframe computers and many legacy companies that specialized in mainframe computing went out of business. On the other hand, the startups that led the personal computing revolution like Apple and Microsoft went on to become some of the most valuable companies on Earth.

However, not all startups choose a low end use case as their initial niche. It's possible to take the opposite strategy and launch an initial product targeted to high end users. This is the strategy that Tesla has taken en route to mass adoption of its electric cars. When Tesla launched the Roadster in 2008, it came with a base price of around $100,000 (which is over $150,000 today after adjusting for inflation). The Tesla Roadster received exceptional reviews from the major auto magazines, but very few people could afford it. Tesla's most affordable option for the mass market, the Model 3, was announced 8 years later at much less than half the price. Tesla reportedly sold only 2,500 Roadsters, but they've sold over 1 million Model 3s.

As a startup, it's usually a terrible idea to go after a large market with your first product. Many entrepreneurs confuse their first product with their vision. Your vision should be huge, but your first product should only target a small fraction of the customers you hope to gain eventually. If your vision is to sell a single product, it's way too small. Instead, you should think in terms of a series of products, in which each successive product is a step towards achieving your vision. Deciding what your first product should be is one of the most important decisions you'll have to make, because the niche you choose to invade first will determine if you can gain a solid foothold in the market that you can leverage to accelerate your pace of innovation.

There are two ways to think about the problem of identifying your initial niche. Your niche determines how your product should differentiate itself from other options. And, the way your product is differentiated determines its niche. You can work backwards from the niche, or forwards from your differentiators. Given that this is a general book aimed at first time founders in a variety of areas, it's difficult to write this chapter by working backwards by starting with a market and dividing it up into niches in a way that applies to everyone. However, there are generally only a few ways to differentiate your product that apply across all contexts, so I'll focus on those.

At a high level, there are only four levers for developing a differentiated product. You can build your product based on a proprietary technology that only you can use. You can design a product to create a much better user experience than other options. You can provide exceptional customer service. Or, you can offer your product at a lower price than alternatives. Usually, companies choose some combination of these levers to develop a differentiated product.

Deep technology companies typically choose to differentiate by developing a proprietary technology. The development of this technology generally requires substantial up-front R&D expenditures. In addition, it usually takes many years to make sufficient progress in R&D before the company can even release its first product. The benefit to the business is that developing a proprietary technology can provide the company with a durable long-term advantage over potential competitors. In fact, it can open completely unexplored markets, enabling the business to command high prices, and may even provide the company with a short term monopoly in those new markets. This is essentially a first-mover's advantage. Moreover, the societal benefits of novel technologies are often profound and often underestimated in the long term. There's a lot to like about deep technology companies for people courageous enough to take this path.

That said, there are a number of significant challenges to building deep technology companies. Obviously, it's possible that the R&D efforts simply fail, the technology doesn't work, and the company goes out of business without ever releasing a product. This happens all the time to biotech startups. Even if we put that aside, however, there are still significant hurdles. First, customers are often hesitant to rely on novel technologies. As a result, products released by deep technology companies often face skepticism and slow rates of adoption, even if the technology works exceptionally well. Second, the relatively slow rate of adoption of products based on novel technologies means that it can be difficult to get useful product feedback from customers. Third, the long time required for R&D and the time needed to overcome the skepticism to new technologies in the market combine such that it can take a very long time for deep technology companies to earn substantial revenue or become profitable. In my opinion, the advantages to differentiating on technology outweigh the disadvantages, as long as you and your team are prepared for them. But, if you hire a nervous team of weak people, or people motivated solely by financial metrics, then your team will implode before you reach the promised land. To combat this, you need to make sure that you're only hiring people who are willing to run through walls to achieve the huge vision, and you need to target your first product at early adopters rather than the entire market. Thus, disruption with a deep technology company involves introducing a product that the majority of the market views as 'too early', using tech forward early adopters to generate proof points and get product feedback, and then launching subsequent versions of the product aimed at successively larger segments of the overall market.

A second strategy is to differentiate on product design rather than on the underlying technology. When done well, this strategy is only slightly easier than following the path of deep technology. That's because great product design is really difficult! In my opinion, the best example of a company that has done amazingly well following this strategy is Apple. Apple is renowned for creating products that are exceptionally well designed, not for inventing incredibly innovative technologies. The desktop-based graphical user interface was invented by Xerox and productized by Apple. Smartphones like the Blackberry were on the market for years before Apple released the iPhone. Apple's products aren't really new, they're just better. On the other hand, there's a long list of startups that have failed by building on someone else's technology—the current crop of GPT-wrapper startups has many examples. If you are building on someone else's technology, then there's no barrier to entry for competitors and the only way to be successful is to have a product so well designed that it stands out amongst a sea of similar products. Over time, this can develop into a durable advantage only through the creation of brand equity, when customers associate your brand with high quality. Founders who choose to differentiate on product design often find most success by launching their first product for a high end or luxury market, much like Tesla did with the Roadster. Disruption happens top down. Once the company has established a reputation for great design, it can expand into other market segments by releasing lower priced products. However, they have to be careful not to erode their brand equity in the process.

A third strategy a startup can take is to differentiate based on customer service. Personally, I don't think this is usually a good strategy for a startup. It's too tempting to wander down the pathway of becoming a consulting company, optimizing for short term revenue without building any durable advantage at all. Your costs will be astronomical, your margins will be low, and your company will not be valued as highly as other technology-based companies. Nevertheless, it is possible. As a customer service focused startup, your initial niche has to be small because you will not have the capacity to provide high quality services to many customers. The path to expanding to the broader market is likely through automation. By automating as much as possible, you aim to provide the same high quality experience for your customers at a much lower cost than your competitors. Much as for startups that aim to differentiate through design, the primary durable advantage will be brand equity. However, there is a possibility that infrastructure and trade secrets, which allow you to provide your services at a larger scale and at lower cost than your competitors, will provide an advantage too. Disruption of existing solutions happens as you remove barriers to scale; think of Amazon expanding from selling only books to becoming the everything store.

The final strategy is to differentiate yourself from potential competitors by offering lower priced solutions. A few conditions need to be present in order for this strategy to work. First, the broader market you're targeting must have a large number of customers. For example, it would be difficult to follow a low price strategy if you are targeting large enterprise customers in, say, the Fortune 500. However, such a strategy could make sense if you are targeting all small businesses in the United States. You need to make up for lower prices through high volume. Typically, your startup would introduce a low priced product targeting low end customers. Then, you would hope to use automation and leverage economies of scale as you grow, to enable you to move up market and offer your low priced products to more consumers. This is the typical disruption story relayed in anecdotes such as the personal computer revolution.

One aspect of these strategies for differentiation that isn't discussed frequently is that they are path dependent. If you start your company by developing a differentiated technology or by investing substantial resources in product design, you'll probably end up launching a high priced product but there's nothing stopping you from lowering your prices later on. However, if you start by launching a low priced product that isn't based on a differentiated technology, then you will likely never launch a product based on a differentiated technology. As a result, I believe that it is almost always best in the long run to aim for developing a differentiated technology and great product design.

21. Manage to your advantage

There are two competing myths about good management that Paul Graham called "founder mode" and "manager mode". In founder mode, the leader of a company or organization stays deep in the details, they keep their hands on the wheel and steer the company towards achieving their vision themselves. In manager mode, the leader instead describes their vision to others, and then takes their hands off the wheel, trusting their employees to steer them towards achieving their vision without much oversight. The founder says, "get busy micro-managing, or get busy dying–that's goddamn right." The manager says, "in order to lead, get out of the way". Both are wrong, or perhaps both are right.

I used to describe my management style as The Eye of Sauron. The metaphor was meant to be somewhat self-deprecating, but also illustrative. The Eye has a focused gaze. And, when it focuses on something, it sees everything that's going on in that area and brings with it an unmatched intensity. These attributes are good things for leaders to bring to their areas of comparative advantage. But, The Eye also shifts its gaze from one area to another. It gets distracted. And this distraction ultimately leads to its downfall. In keeping with the metaphor, I would focus on one area of the company at a time–whatever I thought was our biggest problem or opportunity–digging into the details, getting my hands dirty, and bringing a sense of urgency and intensity. And, I would shift my area of focus periodically to make sure it aligned with our top priority at the time. As a first time founder, I thought this was a good idea because it always highlighted what was important, but I now realize that this philosophy caused me to dig into the details in areas outside of my comparative advantage, areas where I paid a high opportunity cost.

The Eye of Sauron method of management violates the principle of comparative advantage because it encourages a leader to spend too much time outside of their areas of relative strength. Likewise, manager mode violates the principle of comparative advantage because it encourages a leader to spend too little time within their areas of relative strength. The correct path is to behave in founder mode within your areas of comparative advantage, and to behave in manager mode outside them. Get hands-on in your strongest areas, and delegate your weakest areas.

In many ways, this seems like the obviously correct approach to leadership. "Lean into your strengths, and delegate your weaknesses," sounds like common sense, not sage contrarian advice. So, why isn't this advice standard? Why are so many founders told to mold themselves to the CEO role, rather than to mold the role to themselves?

I have two hypotheses, with a similar origin story. Many more people have experience rising up through the leadership ranks at big companies than running startups. As a result, most books on management describe the perspective of someone at these big companies, where a leader is slotting into an existing organizational structure with predefined roles. They do not cover the startup scenario in which the founder has the opportunity to define all of those roles however they want. My first hypothesis is that too many founders are listening to advice from their investors or boards. Fewer venture capitalists than you would think have experience building their own startups, so they get their knowledge by reading management books. Then, these venture capitalists invest in startups, sit on the board of directors, and advise (and sometimes pressure) their founders to grow up and "behave like a CEO". It's true that startup boards often include one or two independent directors in addition to founders and investors, but these independent directors are often chosen from the leadership ranks at large companies, which comes with the same problem. My second hypothesis is that the founder caves to pressure from their employees to get out of the weeds and focus only on executive business tasks. This tends to happen at the Vice President stage when the founder inadvertently starts to hire people afflicted with manageritis, sometimes from big companies but always well-versed in leadership advice from the most well-known management books.

If those are the causes, then the solutions are quite simple. The founder just needs the discipline to follow a few guidelines (which, to be honest, isn't usually easy even if they are simple). First, the founder needs to define their areas of comparative advantage, and define the CEO role at their company as including them. Second, the founder needs to write this down in a document they share with new investors and employees, while those people are still deciding if they want to join the company or not. Third, the founder should only hire people that fit their style and agree to the way the founder defined their role as CEO, especially in leadership roles. Fourth, the founder should stay hands-on within their areas of comparative advantage, acting as a player/coach and dedicating at least 2 days per week to individual contributor work. Fifth, the founder should delegate areas outside of their comparative advantage to trusted leaders, and hold them strictly accountable for any results they commit to delivering (that is, get rid of them if they fail to deliver a result they committed to). And, finally, the founder should never cave to pressure from their board or employees to delegate their areas of strength, or to dive into the weeds in their weakest areas.

If you follow these simple guidelines, you'll avoid both traps of founder and manager mode.

Unfortunately, most first time founders find it difficult to hold leaders accountable outside of their areas of comparative advantage. One reason is that priorities change frequently at a startup. If a leader commits to delivering a result and simply fails to do so, or does this frequently, then it's pretty clear what to do—move them out. But, if a leader commits to delivering a result, but doesn't deliver the result because the company's priorities shifted mid-project, then it's hardly fair (or a good idea) to fire them for that. First time founders often give their leaders too many chances, however, not too few. One reason for this, I think, is that it feels risky to fire someone from your leadership team, like it will create a leadership vacuum that will cause chaos throughout the organization. To avoid this, it's a good idea for a founder to have a succession plan ready to go for each of their leaders. You should know who you'll ask to move into the role if you decide to make a leadership change, whether or not they will do so permanently or on an interim basis, and how you'll conduct a search for a permanent replacement if necessary. Having the plan in place will make it easier to make the decision if and when the time comes. In addition, each member of the leadership team should set committed goals each quarter that are in service to their primary objective. Within an Objectives and Key Results (OKR) framework, one might call these committed goals "key results" but I think that "committed goals" is more clear. That is, each team has one high level objective and two or three committed goals that they would need to achieve in order to meet the objective. These committed goals should be written down, so they can be reviewed at the end of the quarter. A goal is either hit, missed, or deprioritized; and the latter requires you to sign off during the quarter when the decision to change priorities was made. If someone fails to meet their committed goals after one quarter, see how you feel, but if they do so for two quarters in a row you need to let them go.

I advocate that founder/CEOs should stay hands on within their areas of comparative advantage even as their company grows. There are a few ways to do this. The first way is that the founder dedicates two days per week to hands-on work within their area of comparative advantage. For example, if the founder is an incredible product designer they could spend Mondays and Tuesdays, or Tuesdays and Thursdays, or Thursdays and Fridays working on design. Whichever two days they prefer. A second way is that the founder dedicates three to four hours per day to hands-on work within their area of comparative advantage. For example, the founder could spend 8:30am to 12:30pm getting hands-on with design work each day. In fact, this is roughly the strategy taken by fashion designer and entrepreneur Brunello Cucinelli, who spends his morning on design work and his afternoons on other aspects of the business.[1] A third approach is to have everything all mixed up— one hour on this task, 30 minutes on another—rather than continuous blocks for deep focused work. I do not think this third strategy is very good, but many entrepreneurs fall into this trap if they aren't disciplined about saying no to requests during their dedicated work blocks. Whatever you decide on, you need to protect your work blocks with the intensity of a trained Doberman.

Founder/CEOs face two issues when it comes to scheduling time to stay hands-on in their areas of comparative advantage. The first, as mentioned above, is that there will be many demands for their time from other parts of the company, as well as from external parties. Protecting your time from other parts of your company is easier than protecting it from external parties; after all, it seems sensible to take meetings with

----

1. https://www.harpersbazaar.com/fashion/designers/a17874/brunello-cucinelli-profile/

customers or investors according to their schedules, rather than your own. This tends to be less of a challenge if you schedule your work blocks as entire days, such as Tuesdays and Thursdays, than if you choose a daily work block, such as from 8:30am to 12:30pm each day. It's uncommon that someone is unavailable for 3 days per week, every week, but it's relatively common for someone to be unavailable at the same time every day. This is especially true if you're taking meetings with people in many time zones. However, the ability to schedule time with external parties isn't your only consideration. You'll likely have other team members working on projects within your area of comparative advantage with whom you'll need to coordinate your activities. It's easier to slot into a project team if you are working on it every day than if you only work on it two days per week. Thus, neither choice is strictly better than the other. If you have to take many external meetings, then I suggest dedicating two full days per week to deep work. But, if you have to coordinate your deep work with other team members then I suggest dedicating a few hours to that work every day.

In my first job as a founder/CEO, I had a lot of demands for my time from external parties like customers, investors, and journalists. As a result, I aimed to dedicate two days per week to my area of comparative advantage (i.e., to technology R&D). To be honest, I spread myself too thin and often found myself in category three, trying to context switch back and forth throughout the day. Not good. Nevertheless, I found one way of doing deep work—in particular, work on projects that require collaboration—that I found effective. I call this "berserk mode".

"Berserk mode" is one of my preferred methods for working on projects. It can be used for deep work within your areas of comparative advantage, or it can help you bang out some boring stuff that you would procrastinate otherwise. Going into berserk mode involves four things:

1. Choose a time window (maximum one day) during which you'll work on only one task.
2. Decide what needs to be finished at the end of that time window. There must be an output.
3. Accept that perfect is the enemy of good and that failure is not an option.
4. Work non-stop like your life depends on it during the time window to finish the task.

Berserk mode is a great tool for "gettin' shit done" because if you do it right you cannot fail to get shit done.

Berserk mode was born because I hate responding to my emails. As a result, they kept piling up until I couldn't take it anymore. So, I would set aside a block of time – say, 3 hours – and I'd say "at the end of this 3 hours I need to have responded to or deleted every single email in my inbox." Then, I would just do it. A hundred emails to go through? Who cares? Just get it done.

Berserk mode is not something you can do every day because it should be intense. It is especially helpful for tasks you (or your team) are going to procrastinate on. By the way, procrastination in the corporate environment doesn't always look like it did for your high school homework; instead, it often takes the form of something that looks like work, but is not work--discussion. Every corporate person's favorite way to procrastinate on doing real work is to engage in endless discussion. "But how should we do it?" they will say, "we need to set up a meeting to plan and get alignment." By now you probably recognize this as the early stages of manageritis. Stop it! Just do a berserk mode and just get that shit done.

Berserk mode is great for teams who are prone to too much discussion and consensus building because you simply have to finish the task in the time you've set aside for it. You cannot leave until the task is complete, and you'll be surprised at how much quicker you get commitment to action when everyone understands that.

Berserk mode is a good way to stand up a prototype or a first draft, but often won't take you all the way. Though, you'll be surprised at how far you can get with a half day of focused effort. However, "perfect is the enemy of good" is one of the key berserk mode principles, so you will probably have to go back to edit and fine tune the outcome of your berserk mode in the days following.

Berserk mode is also useful as a tool for molding your company's culture. It forces people to be decisive, to have a sense of urgency, to focus on the highest priority item, and to avoid perfectionism. At least for one day. In my opinion, it's also pretty fun. Sort of like taking a difficult exercise class with some friends, but it's exercising your brain instead of your body. By going berserk every once in a while, you can train yourself and your colleagues to kick it into a higher gear.

22. Keep meetings to a minimum

Most people spend vastly too much of their lives in meaningless meetings. Every second that you or one of your employees is in a meeting is one second something important isn't getting done. Nobody should be using meetings to give updates. You can give someone updates on the status of a project over email or slack. There are only a few types of meetings that are worth having.

First, I do not believe in recurring one-on-one meetings between managers and their direct reports. Belief in the utility of weekly one-on-ones is a clear symptom of manageritis. There are only two good reasons to have a one-on-one with a direct report. There may be a sensitive issue to discuss that either you or your direct report are uncomfortable discussing in a group setting. Such issues should be rare, however, which means that a recurring meeting is not necessary and issues can be handled by ad-hoc meetings at the request of either party. If someone is frequently having issues that need to be discussed in private, then there is a problem. You are not going to fix the problem by talking about it in your weekly one-on-one. Instead, you need to go investigate the problem to get to its root cause and fix that. The other reason to have a one-on-one is just to chat, build your relationship. I don't think a weekly recurring meeting is a good way to do that. Instead, I suggest periodically going for a coffee, grabbing a drink after work, or going for a walk. Keep the purpose of the meeting in mind, that it's basically just for socializing. Don't set up recurring one-on-one meetings.

A second type of meeting that is useful is a brainstorm. Brainstorms often need to be a couple of hours long. They should focus on a single topic. Never try to brainstorm two or more topics at once or you'll end up brainstorming on nothing. The topic of the brainstorm should be provided to the participants ahead of time, and they should write out some ideas before coming to the meeting without talking to each other. Then, you can use the meeting to put all of the ideas together, see if any other ideas come to mind, and then debate the advantages and disadvantages of the various ideas. If the goal of the meeting is to select one idea to move forward with, make sure it's clear at the outset who is responsible for making that decision. It must be a single person in the meeting. In some cases, you may want the person responsible for choosing the idea to move forward with to avoid offering up any of their own ideas. That is, you have three or four people generating ideas and debating their pros and cons, and then one person who is acting as the judge to select the best idea.

A third type of meeting that is useful is a meeting to make a decision. A good way to run a meeting in which a key decision will be made is to have someone prepare a memo with all of the necessary context prior to the meeting. Then, have the three or four participants spend the first 15 minutes of the meeting reviewing the memo in silence. Once everybody has read the memo, you can spend some time debating what should be done. As above, one person should be designated as the person responsible for making the decision. This should be clear from the outset. Once all of the arguments have been made, this person should decide. Everybody else must commit to following through on their decision, even if they disagree with it. Consensus is the enemy of speed and a killer of progress. The person who made the decision should revise the memo to state what decision they've made and why.

A fourth type of meeting that is useful is a meeting for feedback or user testing. In such a meeting, someone will be responsible for bringing a prototype. The other participants will be responsible for providing feedback on the prototype. In some cases, this could be done offline because the users can check out the prototype and then write down their feedback. But a lot of great feedback is non-verbal, and someone who is observant or skilled in user testing will gain at least as much information out of watching how people interact with and respond to the prototype than what they say about it. It is usually helpful to record these meetings.

And, the fifth type of useful meeting is one to inform or rally the troops as a whole. In general, I think it's much better to inform individuals or small groups through writing. However, this doesn't work well for large groups because, inevitably, some significant fraction of people in the group simply won't read your memo. Rather than asking all of the employees at your company to read some memo so that they know what is going on, it's much easier to just gather them up for an all-hands and tell them. Every time you gather a large group like that together, make sure you use the occasion to reiterate your mission and why it's important before you get into anything else. This reinforces that the mission is the most important thing, your North Star. In addition, after you extol the importance of the mission, highlight the company's highest priority at the moment. This reinforces your ruthless prioritization. Only after you've done these things should you move on to other business.

I recommend having a recurring meeting with your leadership team every week. This meeting belongs to the fifth type. You should kick off the meeting every single week by talking about the mission and vision, and what you think is the most important thing for the company to be focused on right now. Next, have each person in your leadership team present (i) the thing that is going best on their team right now (i.e., the good news), (ii) the thing that is going worst on their team right now (i.e., the bad news), and (iii) their team's number one priority right now. At the end of the meeting, you should decide if any of the items merit follow up meetings for brainstorming solutions or making decisions. Don't use your recurring meeting for that purpose, always set up another meeting for the brainstorm or to make the decision.

I also recommend having regular town halls and all-hands meetings. These also belong to the fifth type of meeting. Kick off the meeting as described above, but then transition into a back and forth conversation with your employees. Don't take anonymous questions, because anonymity makes people act stupidly. Keep things conversational. It can be helpful to limit the size of the groups so that people feel more comfortable speaking up. I suggest holding one town hall every week with a small group of people from around your company, and one town hall every month with the entire company.

As a general rule, an in person meeting is 10x better than a virtual meeting. Therefore, you want to try to have every participant in a meeting there in-person. One time, I recall one of my co-founders and I going back and forth about a particular technical problem over Slack for a week or two until we eventually decided we had to make time to discuss it at a whiteboard. Then, we solved the problem in 20 minutes. Being in-person is also necessary to enable collisions. Collisions are spontaneous interactions you have when you bump into one of your colleagues at the coffee machine, sit down for lunch with your team, or notice someone writing something interesting on a whiteboard and pop your head in to check it out. You cannot replicate these collisions remotely, and they are a crucial part of team building, communication, and innovation.

When the story came out that Jensen Huang does not have one-on-ones with his direct reports at Nvidia, one of the first questions people raised was "how does he give feedback?" The answer is that he often gives feedback in a group setting. I believe that most feedback, both positive and negative, should be given in a group setting. For positive feedback, this isn't very controversial. Most people like to be recognized for a job well done. But, it's quite controversial for negative feedback. However, if one person has made a mistake, it's likely that others have or will make that same mistake too. Correcting the mistake in a group setting makes sure that everybody learns the lesson.

General Patton believed in giving feedback immediately, and usually publicly. His officers would often push back and tell him that all the best management books of the time said this was poor practice (the disease of manageritis caused by people listening to the advice of armchair leadership experts has been with humanity a long time). In return, he would ask them something like "What happens if you touch a live electric wire?" They would say, "well, you get shocked, of course." "Exactly! And, how long after you touch the wire do you feel the shock?" Patton would probe. The reply would come, "Immediately". "Right again!" Patton would go on, "In war, a mistake can get a man killed. Or worse, one man's mistake could get hundreds of other men killed. There is no point in trying to save the ego of a man if the man is dead. A dead man has no ego!" [1] Thankfully, people aren't usually killed in the general course of business at a startup. But people do lose their jobs. At a big company with a long history of profitability, one person's mistake may hurt the bottom line a bit, but at a startup one person's mistake can cause the company to go out of business. Most startups are teetering on the edge of oblivion. One person's mistake can cause everybody to lose their jobs. If you want to build a great startup, you can't be in the business of protecting your employees' egos.

---

1. General Patton's Principles for Life & Leadership by Porter B. Williamson

23. The first version always sucks

Many quotes attributed to famous historical figures are actually made up. Sometimes they are entirely made up, sometimes they are misattributed, sometimes they are taken out of context, and sometimes they paraphrase a longer, more nuanced argument from the purported author. For example, there doesn't appear to be any written evidence that Albert Einstein ever said the exact quote, "Everything should be made as simple as possible, but not simpler." [1] Although this is a brilliant aphorism, it appears that this line was written by somebody else in an attempt to distill the essence of a longer lecture given by Einstein. This chapter is inspired by a quote, often attributed to Henry Ford, that may be similarly manufactured, but is equally wise, "If I had asked people what they wanted, they would have said faster horses." [2]

----

1. https://quoteinvestigator.com/2011/05/13/einstein-simple/#google_vignette
2. https://hbr.org/2011/08/henry-ford-never-said-the-fast

Some people seem to believe that the purpose of a startup is to make money by creating a product that people want, and then selling it to them. This can lead one down a path of customer driven product development, rather than vision driven product development. I do not believe in customer driven product development. Simply asking potential customers what they would like you to build always leads to building a complete piece of shit. Always. If the customer already knew what solution they wanted, they would have already built it themselves! Your job as an entrepreneur is to have a vision! To go out on a limb and experiment to find out if your vision resonates with the rest of the world. Not to just build some crappy product to make a few bucks. That's not to say I don't believe in using customer feedback, of course I do. But, feedback should be used to refine the details of the product not to set the vision.

I've seen entrepreneurs take two paths under the broader umbrella that I call visionary product development, depending on what their vision is. The first path, which people sometimes refer to as a 'market pull', often occurs when the entrepreneur's vision revolves around solving a particular customer problem —often one they experienced for themselves. The second path, which people sometimes refer to as a 'market push', often occurs when the entrepreneur's vision revolves around inventing and developing a particular technology. Many business book authors advise founders to fall in love with the problem rather than the solution because people perceive a 'market pull' to be a bit easier than a 'market push', but I don't think that advice makes sense. Your vision is the thing that inspires you to take the leap, to run through walls, to be relentless in spite of the ups-and-downs of the startup rollercoaster.

You fall in love with what you fall in love with. You can't choose to fall in love with something because you think it will be easier. What inspires you is about you—not about your customers. If you go after a 'market pull' that you don't find exciting, and so give up before you reach the summit, then your startup will fail. If you go after a 'market push' and can't find the right problem to solve with your invention, then your startup will fail. You can fail either way. At least in the latter case, you will fail trying to do something you believe in.

If your vision revolves around solving a particular customer problem—that is, there is near zero uncertainty that your customers would love to purchase a product that solves this problem, and that the market is big enough to support a venture scale startup—then you are primarily taking on technical and execution risk. The question is, "what should the solution look like?" Given that your customers are probably smart people, and also assuming that this problem is well-known to other would-be entrepreneurs, it must mean that there's no obvious solution to the problem. Since the problem is clear, and its solution is valuable, someone would have solved it already if the solution was obvious. For example, suppose your vision is to cure cancer. Everybody—literally every single person on earth—would purchase a cure for cancer if it existed (and if they could afford it). The challenge is that nobody knows how to discover such a thing. Therefore, product development under a 'market pull' vision typically requires the founder to work backwards from the bigger problem in order to break it down into a series of smaller problems that seem more tractable.

If your vision revolves around a new technology or invention —that is, there is near zero technical risk because you've already built the initial technology—then you are primarily taking on market and execution risk. The question is, "what important and valuable problem can this technology help solve?" For example, recent developments in artificial intelligence have led to the invention of large language models, and hundreds of startups have been born trying to use this new technology to create compelling products. The challenge is that nobody knows if the technology will be good enough to solve a truly important problem yet. Therefore, product development under a 'market push' vision typically requires the founder to explore an idea maze of potential applications of their technology to find the optimal match between the capabilities of the technology and the requirements of the problem.

As you can see, I don't think that 'market pull' and 'market push' visions tend to be particularly different. In both cases, the founders need to spend a lot of their time exploring the landscape of problems, and their success usually depends on picking the right problem to attack first. If you pick the right problem and the right technology, you'll have a chance at success (there's still execution risk, so success isn't guaranteed). But, if you pick either the wrong problem or the wrong technology, you'll have little chance for long term success unless you can execute a large pivot in flight. There is a caveat that you may be able to achieve short term success if you pick the right problem but the wrong technology, in which case you'll get some initial traction but will have poor customer retention, or the wrong problem with a powerful new technology, in which case you may be able to raise substantial venture capital but will fail to get strong traction with customers.

In any case, picking the right first problem is the hard part. A journey of 1000 miles begins with a single step, but it's the first step that's most dangerous.

Overall, my product philosophy is captured by the following five principles. Given that I believe that 'market pull' and 'market push' visions are generally pretty similar, I think these principles can apply to either case.

Push boundaries.

I believe in creating products that push the boundaries both of what your customers believe is possible and of current techno-logical capabilities. It's very difficult to create a world changing startup by following convention, you need to do something original.

Create opinionated designs.

I believe that the best products are built by people who have a deep empathy for a customer's problems and an utter disregard for their proposed solutions. Instead of listening to what a customer says they want, you are better off internalizing their problem and then building a product that you would want if you were in their shoes. I believe that product designers, product managers, and engineers should form strong opinions about what will make the product great.

Build simple user experiences.

I believe that technologically advanced products require super simple user experiences or potential customers will be too scared to try them. The best products have a crystal clear and concrete value proposition, but a product that provides a clean, elegant, and intuitive user experience is magical. There are many financially successful products with terrible user experiences, particularly enterprise products, but I couldn't look myself in the mirror if I were working on one (and not trying desperately to redesign it).

Rapidly iterative in development.

Just because you've chosen a compelling vision doesn't mean you'll realize it on your first try. In fact, if you do achieve your vision on your first try, then your vision certainly wasn't big enough. Your first version will suck. It will not come close to achieving your vision, and your customers will find lots of things they don't like about it. I believe it's necessary to go through multiple iterations on a product before it will actually be great, and that it's impossible to shortcut this process with any amount of planning. Therefore, one should be decisive in forming strong opinions about the product, build it quickly, test it with customers, and repeat. Up front market research is a poor guide to product development, but user feedback on a prototype or launched product is incredibly valuable. Don't confuse the two.

Stay on the path towards a bigger vision.

Achieving your vision is like being the first person to summit an unclimbed mountain. The products you launch as you build your startup are like the camps a climber sets up along the way. You adjust your path based on feedback from the market, just like a climber adjusts their path to go around unforeseen obstacles or deal with unfavorable weather conditions. But it doesn't matter how great your basecamp was if you end up climbing the wrong mountain! I believe that founders should only build products that align with their North Star, that take them closer to realizing their vision. If a product doesn't align with that mission, even if it would be a super successful product, then it's for someone else to build.

In practice, it's helpful to break your bigger vision down into a series of products. You should write a memo that lays out—at a high level, you don't need details (and can't know them yet anyway)—what these products will be and how they'll lay out the path to achieving your vision. The most famous example of such a memo is "The Secret Tesla Motors Master Plan (just between you and me)" by Elon Musk. [3] I wrote a similar "secret plan" memo when I was CEO at Unlearn.AI. [4] You should write one too. Both of these examples were posted publicly, but I don't think that's necessary if it makes you uncomfortable. But, you should make reading your secret plan memo a part of onboarding at your company, so that every single employee is familiar with it.

During the early stages of building your company, you'll only actually be working on the first step of your secret plan. By early stages, I generally mean the first 5 years or so. I don't think it's a good idea to try to plan out all the details. Instead, I

---

3. https://www.tesla.com/secret-master-plan
4. https://unlearnai.substack.com/p/top-secret-plan-for-ai-in-medicine

think you should create a prototype. Then, you should show your prototype to people and see what they think of it. If everybody hates your prototype, then you need to go back to the drawing board and create a new prototype. But, if people are intrigued or excited by your prototype, then drive ahead and build a minimum viable product. For a deep technology company that requires significant R&D, quickly could mean two or three years, which is one of the reasons deep tech companies are considered risky. In any case, you should be going as quickly as possible. This stage of your product cycle should be fast paced. You will need to be decisive. Focused. You'll need to resist temptation to pivot, temptation to add more and more features, temptation to over-engineer your product. Your team will probably get into a lot of disagreements; there will be friction, and there will be long hours. It will be stressful. Then, launch your product! Ship it! Don't wait for it to be perfect, because even if you think it's perfect you'll probably be wrong. If you're uncomfortable shipping it out to all potential customers, then do a limited release. But, you have to get your MVP in front of your customers as quickly as you can.

Once you've shipped your product, then all you have to do is listen to customers, filter which parts of their feedback are aligned with your vision, and iterate on your product. Simple, but not easy.

Part Four
Protocols

You want a hot body? You want a Bugatti?
You want a Maserati? You better work, bitch
You want a Lamborghini? Sip martinis?
Look hot in a bikini? You better work, bitch
You wanna live fancy? Live in a big mansion?
Party in France?
You better work bitch, you better work bitch
You better work bitch, you better work bitch
Now get to work, bitch! (ah-ah)
Now get to work, bitch! (ah-ah)

Britney Spears

24. Practical steps

1. Write a paragraph describing your big vision. Often, you can start with an idea for a concrete product and keep expanding outward until you come up with a world changing concept.
2. Figure out which areas of your startup you want to focus on by analyzing your areas of comparative advantage or unique expertise. I suggest keeping your list to a maximum of three areas.
3. Create a short, colorful description of your personality. Something roughly three paragraphs in length. A simple way to do this is to take an online personality test (such as the Big Five traits) and then ask a language model to craft a description of your personality based on the results.
4. Use the description of your personality profile to write a couple paragraphs describing your preferred working environment. A language model can help do this from your personality profile.

5. Draft a couple of paragraphs describing your personal values, making sure to capture both your core values and the principles that define your sense of aesthetics. You can use the questionnaire in Chapter 4 to help you.

6. Create a list of five traits that you look for in people you tend to work well with, and five traits that predict you're likely to clash with somebody.

7. Take what you've written about your personality traits, your preferred working environment, and your values, and translate them into five cultural principles for your company. Make each of these cultural principles memorable and actionable. They should describe behaviors, not beliefs.

8. Create a personal "user guide" that introduces your company and yourself. For your company, describe the vision and cultural principles. For yourself, provide your areas of expertise, a description of your personality, your preferred working environment, your values, and traits and anti-traits that predict if you're likely to work well with someone. Make sure to provide this user guide to all candidates as part of every job offer.

9. Create a list of all the roles (not job titles) that your startup will need covered during the first year. In the beginning, each person will have to fill multiple roles. Revise the list annually.

10. Identify potential co-founders who share your vision and fit into your cultural principles. Set up the company so that the CEO gets 51% of the initial equity,

and the rest of the equity is split equally among the other founders.

11. Create a cultural assessment to be used for all interviews. Keep the assessment to three questions, and create a clear grading rubric. Have an independent person conduct each culture interview while blind to the candidate's resume. Only candidates that pass the culture interview can move forward, without exception.

12. Check references before sending a written offer to every new hire. To do this, have the candidate provide three references; preferably previous managers or direct reports. Call their references and ask them to rate the candidate from 1 to 10 based on how they compare to others in that role. Also, ask the reference to go through the cultural assessment for the candidate.

13. Create a 90-day check in for all candidates using a peer review system to assess their performance and their culture fit after one quarter in the role. Have your legal counsel put in relevant language about this 90-day check in into your standard offer letter. Get rid of anyone who fails the 90 day check in.

14. Use market data to make sure you're compensating your employees competitively; at least, competitively with other startups of a similar stage. Every employee should receive equity in your startup, and it's better to lean towards more equity at the early stage.

15. Create a framework for the transparent sharing of information with all of your employees who've passed their 90 day check in. Share your metrics, key

performance indicators, good news, and bad news
with all employees.

16. Only raise money around key inflection points that
provide some type of objective validation for your
business. At the earliest stages, this would probably be
when you have a prototype you can show to investors
or, in the case of a deep tech company, could be
something like a scientific paper illustrating a new
invention.

17. Start building relationships with venture capitalists
before you need money. And, after you raise money,
immediately get back to building relationships with
potential investors. By building relationships outside
of your fundraising cycle, you can focus on making
sure the investors are a good fit for your company.

18. In order to raise capital, you will need to create four
pieces of collateral. First, you'll need a non-
confidential deck that describes your vision, why your
team is uniquely qualified to achieve it, and how big it
will be if you do. Second, you'll need a confidential
deck that provides financial information and
projections, customer information, and other details.
Third, you'll need a financial model that projects your
revenue and expenses for approximately three years.
At the early stages, these are just a guess but you'll
need them anyway. Finally, you'll need to set up a data
room with all of these items, plus important legal
documents and contracts. Use the non-confidential
deck to figure out which investors are interested, then
use the rest of the collateral to dive in deeper with
investors under a non-disclosure agreement.

19. Aim to get term sheets from at least two lead investors so that you have a choice. Don't accept a term sheet from an investor who you know is a bad fit for your company; even if you need the money this will come back to bite you in the ass. Figure out some other way to stay alive until you can find a better fit.

20. Set up quarterly board meetings. Provide all of the background information to the board a week ahead of time in a memo, not a slide deck. Err on the side of providing too much context. Keep the board meeting focused on high level strategic questions, and drive the discussion toward two or three topics you want the board to help with. Take any advice from board members as advice coming from a smart person who only knows a little bit about your business, rather than advice from an oracle that you need to listen to.

21. Resist the urge to create detailed plans. Instead, come up with three strategic principles that people throughout your company can use to come up with their own plans. Make sure every employee at your company can describe the vision, cultural and strategic principles.

22. Your company can only have one top priority. Figure out what that is, and make sure every employee knows it. Force every employee to focus on a single thing at a time. Don't let anyone multitask, they can move on to the next item once they finish with their current top priority. Solve all big problems by breaking them down into smaller chunks, and solving each chunk sequentially.

23. Never let a team have more than four people on it. And, make sure that one person on each team is designated as the team leader and that they are in command.

24. Stay in the details within your area of expertise, forever. Don't dive into the details outside of your areas of expertise. Outside of the usual "CEO stuff", spend 40% of your time on the details within your area of expertise. Schedule time for this, and protect that time at all costs.

25. Don't have recurring one-on-ones. Give most feedback, both positive and negative, immediately and in a group setting. Only have ad-hoc one-on-ones for discussion of particularly sensitive issues.

26. Set up a weekly meeting with your leadership team. Start the meeting by reviewing the vision and the company's top priority. Have each person on your leadership team describe their recent highlights, lowlights, and their top priority. Any follow up for brainstorming or decision making resulting from the discussion should happen in a separate dedicated meeting.

27. Hold regular town halls. Start them by reviewing the vision and the company's top priority. Keep the town halls conversational. Don't take anonymous questions. It can be helpful to hold weekly town halls with small groups rather than the whole company to make it more conversational.

28. Keep the number of participants in every meeting to an absolute minimum, just like the number of people on a team.

29. Work with intensity to get to a minimum viable product as quickly as possible. Drive towards this based on intuition and vision, not user research. Ship it, at least as a limited release if you're not comfortable. Then, use customer feedback to iterate on the MVP and make it better.

30. Don't pursue any products that don't align with your vision. Never forget that your vision is the most important thing.

25. Examples

This chapter simply collects a bunch of the examples from throughout the book into one place. Note that these are things that work for me because of my unique combination of skills, personality traits, and values. Yours will almost certainly be different, so just use these as a guide; I don't suggest copying them without significant modification.

Here is an example double sort table used for finding my areas of the business to focus on.

Areas	Importance	Enjoyment	Relative Skill	Total Score
Vision.	1	2	2	5
Research and development.	4	1	3	8
Startup culture.	2	7	1	10
Product.	3	5	4	12
Engineering.	5	3	5	13
Marketing.	7	4	6	17
Sales.	8	6	7	21
Management.	6	8	8	22
Operations.	9	9	9	27
Finance.	10	10	10	30

Here's an example questionnaire that you can use to help elicit your personal values.

Core Values

1. Reflect on a moment when you felt extremely satisfied or proud of something you accomplished. What was it, and what aspects contributed to that feeling?

This question helps identify what brings you fulfillment and the values associated with those accomplishments (e.g., achievement, impact, creativity).

My Answer: I am never extremely satisfied. There is always something that I could have done better, always more to accomplish.

2. Think about a time when you were frustrated or unhappy with a situation at work or in life. What specific factors caused those feelings?

This reveals what you find intolerable or incompatible with your values (e.g., inefficiency, lack of integrity, rigidity).

My Answer: I get frustrated when I've made up my mind about what direction to go, but the people on my team get stuck in indecision. I'd rather flip a coin and adjust course as necessary than sit around and endlessly debate what to do.

3. What activities or tasks make you lose track of time because you're so engaged in them? What do these activities have in common?

Understanding this can highlight your passions and the values they represent (e.g., innovation, problem-solving, helping others).

My Answer: Thinking about science and deriving equations, programming, writing, and building things (i.e., physical things, like construction projections). All these activities involve deeply engaging in creative problem-solving to build or create something new, whether conceptually or physically.

4. Who are three people you deeply admire (they can be people you know personally or public figures), and what qualities do they embody that resonate with you?

This helps you identify values you aspire to, such as leadership, courage, or compassion.

My Answer: Arnold Schwarzenegger once said "The worst thing I could be is just like everyone else. I'd hate that." Elon

Musk embodies the spirit of innovation, relentless drive, and belief in the nearly impossible. Richard Feynman embodied intellectual curiosity, the use of plain language, and disrespect for authority. Interestingly, all three of these people had some flaws, but I can accept the good with the bad.

5. When faced with a difficult decision, what criteria do you usually consider most important?

This uncovers your decision-making priorities and underlying values (e.g., ethical considerations, long-term impact, personal growth).

My Answer: If there are ethical considerations or something like that, then it isn't a difficult decision. Decisions with clear and large consequences are easy to make. Difficult decisions are ones where the consequences are unclear, in which case I trust my gut instinct.

6. Describe a situation where you stood up for something you believed in, even if it was unpopular or risky. What motivated you to do so?

This reveals values you're willing to defend, such as justice, honesty, or innovation.

My Answer: Two things come to mind from my first startup. One is the pursuit of rapid technological innovation in medical research, which is traditionally a very conservative field. The second is the need for relentlessness and intensity when building a startup, that there is no such thing as "work/life balance" for people trying to change the world.

7. What are three things you absolutely cannot tolerate in a professional or personal setting?

Identifying these deal-breakers highlights values that are non-negotiable for you (e.g., dishonesty, disrespect, complacency).

My Answer: Dishonesty and lying is a clear number one. A second is being closed-minded, preventing people from trying new things. A third is lacking courage, particularly when it comes to making difficult decisions or taking action.

8. What types of problems are you naturally drawn to solving, and why do they interest you?

This sheds light on your innate interests and the values they represent (e.g., challenge, creativity, service).

My Answer: I like problems that seem incredibly challenging, preferably people tell me they are nearly impossible, problems that have the potential to change the course of humanity if we can solve them, and problems that require creativity.

9. How do you typically respond to failure or setbacks? Can you provide an example?

Your response can reveal values like resilience, learning, and adaptability.

My Answer: When the going gets tough, the tough get going! I will bulldoze any obstacle put in front of me if that's what's required to achieve my mission.

10. If you could be remembered for one thing after you're gone, what would you want it to be, and why?

This question helps you articulate your ultimate aspirations and core values (e.g., making a difference, pioneering change, kindness).

My Answer: This is a difficult choice between innovation and relentlessness. I suppose I would choose innovation over relentlessness, but it's close.

Aesthetic Principles

1. What is the single most important quality you value in any design (whether it's a product, theory, or artwork)?

This question helps identify the primary aesthetic principle that resonates with you, such as simplicity, functionality, or innovation.

My Answer: I appreciate things that make complex ideas more intuitive and straightforward. To paraphrase Albert Einstein—everything should be made as simple as possible, but not simpler.

2. When you encounter a design you dislike, what's typically the reason?

This reveals the design elements or principles that you find unappealing, highlighting your aesthetic dislikes and possible deal-breakers.

My Answer: I typically dislike things that try to do too much, or serve too many different types of audiences, and end up cluttered and unnecessarily complicated as a result.

3. How do you balance form and function? Do you lean more toward visual appeal or practical effectiveness?

This explores your prioritization between aesthetics and utility, shedding light on how you integrate both in your preferences.

My Answer: If something doesn't work, then I don't like it. Therefore, functionality is the most important thing. But I think the creator should take a stance about which type of functionality is important, and which is not important, and express those opinions through a minimalist design. What you leave out of something is just as important as what you put in.

4. What feeling or experience do you want a design to evoke in its audience or users?

This uncovers the emotional or experiential impact you value in designs, such as inspiration, clarity, or curiosity.

My Answer: I want things to evoke a sense of immediate understanding while also making the audience intrigued to dive in and learn more. So, clarity and curiosity.

5. Do you value innovation over tradition, or vice versa, in design?

This question helps determine your stance on creativity versus conventional approaches within aesthetics.

My Answer: Without question, I value innovation over tradition. The ultimate form of creativity is to come up with something that is simultaneously novel, simple, and useful.

Here is an example "User Guide" that I would use to introduce a hypothetical company and myself (i.e., the founder).

About [Hypothetical Company Name]:

<u>Our Huge Vision</u>

[Hypothetical Example] We will develop energy storage technology so powerful and efficient that it will decouple human civilization from traditional power grids, enabling a sustainable future where every home, vehicle, and city can generate, store, and distribute their own clean energy, revolutionizing global energy independence.

<u>Cultural Principles</u>

Invent or Die

We exist to obliterate conventions, destroy outdated practices, and set new standards. Innovation is our lifeblood, not a department or trend. Creativity and intuition propel us beyond known limits into uncharted territories, where we don't just follow rules—we make them. If it exists, we will reimagine it, improve it, or replace it entirely. Bold risks and unconventional ideas drive us forward because if we're not rewriting the script, we're failing.

Take Immediate Action

We operate with relentless urgency. Bureaucracy, pointless meetings, and hesitation are enemies of progress—we cut through them all to maintain pure focus on immediate results. Action isn't just a preference; it's a mandate. We make bold, instinctive decisions, moving directly from idea to execution. If it doesn't drive us forward now, it doesn't belong. We don't wait for permission; we move, decide, and build now.

Embrace the Battle

We operate with absolute honesty and authenticity. Bullshit and hidden agendas have no place here. Trust is forged through brutal transparency and unwavering integrity.. This is a battleground for the bold. We demand unfiltered honesty and thrive on direct, intense debate. Here, friction is fuel, and only the strongest ideas emerge. Ego is left at the door—there's no room for it when victory demands clear minds and tough skins. We confront challenges head-on, knowing that only through relentless, candid dialogue can we push our ideas to their highest potential. If you can't keep up, don't step up.

Distill to the Core

Complexity is for the unfocused. We cut through the noise, distilling ideas and designs down to their purest, most essential form. Simplicity isn't just beautiful—it's a weapon, a functional imperative that drives relentless impact. Anything unnecessary is discarded; clarity and intuition rule. Genius lies in making the complex feel inevitable, so that every idea, every product, feels as though it could never have been any other way.

Never Relent

We don't chase competitors; we pursue impact. Obstacles are merely fuel, and setbacks only drive us to push harder. We're an unstoppable force, moving relentlessly forward with resilience, grit, and an unbreakable commitment to bend the curve of humanity. When we encounter an obstacle, we say, "Fuck it. We've got this shit." Reaching the summit is just the beginning—once we're there, we're already looking to the horizon for the next mountain to climb.

About the Founder:

In order to understand our company, you need to understand who created it.

My Areas of Focus

- Inventing new technologies and products.
- Telling our story and evangelizing our vision.
- Creating an ambitious, relentless, fast-paced culture.

What I'm Like

I'm not the type to sit back and let things just happen to me. I shape the world around me and take control of outcomes—I'm driven by this deep, unshakable belief that, if something's going to get done, I'm the one who's going to do it.

I'm relentless. I'm not here to tiptoe around comfort zones, mine or anyone else's. I go after big, bold ideas, the kind that make people squirm a little because they can't quite wrap their heads around them. If it's complex, uncharted, or supposedly "impossible," I'm diving into the deep end. I'm driven by the thrill of taking things apart, seeing how they work, and pushing them beyond their limits—because, let's be real, pushing boundaries is where the magic happens. I value intuition as much as data, because data always comes from the past and can only get you what you've already got; it takes creativity to make something new.

I feel a deep seated need to move fast. And, I'm easily frustrated when I think the people around me are moving too slowly, particularly when they can't just make a goddamned decision. When I'm with people, I don't sugarcoat, and I don't dance around issues. I speak my mind, get to the heart of things, and drive us forward. I thrive in environments that let me shake things up, throw my weight behind big ideas, and make shit happen. If it means breaking convention or ruffling feathers, so be it. Some people don't like working with me because they think I'm too intense, but others realize that I'm a passionate, high agency, goal oriented person who cares deeply about doing great work and making the world better. This passion is contagious for the right people. I'm here to leave a mark, and I'm not waiting around for permission.

Do I get anxious? Of course. Stressed out sometimes? You bet. But I get over it quickly. Stress and obstacles are fuel, plain and simple. When the going gets tough, the tough get going.

I've got a passion for new ideas and a restlessness that drives me to leave a mark. If there's an obstacle, I'll bulldoze through it. If there's a limit, I'm going to push past it. I'm an unstoppable force. I'm not here to blend in or go along quietly. I'm here to break ground, move fast, and make damn sure people feel the impact of what I do.

What I Believe

My core values center on a relentless drive and ambition. I'm never fully satisfied and always believe there's more to accomplish. Drawn to incredibly challenging problems that can change humanity, I value innovation over tradition and aim to pioneer impactful solutions. Action and decisiveness are crucial to me; I become frustrated with indecision and prefer making bold choices and adjusting as necessary. Integrity and honesty are non-negotiable. I value open-mindedness and the courage to try new things and make difficult decisions. When faced with obstacles, I push harder to achieve my mission, admiring individuality and those who challenge the status quo.

In terms of aesthetics, I deeply appreciate simplicity and clarity. I value designs that make complex ideas intuitive, adhering to the principle of making things as simple as possible but not simpler. Functionality is paramount; if something doesn't work, it's unacceptable regardless of visual appeal. I believe in minimalist design, recognizing that what is left out is as important as what is included. I have a strong aversion to clutter and overcomplication, preferring innovation over tradition to create something novel, simple, and useful. My aesthetic principles mirror my core values, emphasizing innovation, functionality, and the elegance of simplicity.

How I Work

I thrive in an environment that's as fast-paced and dynamic as I am. Put me in a place where big ideas aren't just welcomed—they're the lifeblood of the operation. I need the freedom to move quickly, take risks, and shake things up without getting tangled in bureaucratic bullshit or red tape. Let's cut the endless meetings and get straight to making things happen.

I want to be surrounded by passionate, high-agency people who aren't afraid to roll up their sleeves and dive headfirst into ambitious projects. Collaboration is key, but so is decisiveness. I can't stand when folks hem and haw over trivial details or can't make a goddamned decision. Let's trust our instincts, make the call, and keep the momentum going.

An open, transparent environment where everyone speaks their mind suits me best. I value candor over politeness—there's no time for tiptoeing around egos when we're aiming to make a real impact. Give me a team that's ready to challenge each other, push boundaries, and isn't afraid to ruffle a few feathers along the way.

Flexibility and adaptability are non-negotiables. Rigid processes and outdated rules just slow us down. If there's a better way to do something, I want the freedom to pursue it—immediately. I value intuition and creativity just as much as data and analytics. Sometimes you have to go with your gut to break new ground.

I need a workspace that's buzzing with energy—a place where challenges are seen as opportunities, and everyone is driven to leave their mark. Stagnation is the enemy. I feed off constant movement, innovation, and the relentless pursuit of excellence.

In short, I flourish in environments that embrace bold thinking, swift action, and unapologetic ambition. Let's skip the small talk and safe bets—I'm here to change the game, and I need a workplace that's ready to do the same.

Compatibility with Others

I tend to work well with people if they exhibit all of the following five traits:

- They are authentic and honest.
- They value innovation and think creatively.
- They are decisive and take quick, bold actions.

- They are mentally tough, and direct in communication.
- They are pragmatic and care about results rather than processes.

If someone exhibits even one of the following traits, I often end up clashing with them:

- They are full of shit.
- They tend to follow convention.
- They are very deliberate and cautious.
- They are very sensitive, or passive aggressive.
- They value theory or process more than impact.

Culture Fit Assessment for a 20-Minute Interview

<u>Instructions for Interviewer:</u>

This concise interview is designed to assess the candidate's alignment with our company's cultural principles. Please ask the following three questions, scoring each from 1 to 5 using the provided rubric. A score below 3 on any question or a total score below 12 out of 15 will result in the candidate's elimination from the selection process.

Important Notes:

- Focus solely on the candidate's cultural fit.
- Encourage specific examples from past experiences.

- Assess innovation, urgency, resilience, simplicity, authenticity, and direct communication.
- Use the rubrics consistently for objective scoring.

Time Management:

- Introduction: 2 minutes
- Each Question: 5 minutes (total of 15 minutes)
- Candidate's response: ~3 minutes
- Follow-up questions: ~2 minutes
- Closing: 3 minutes

Question 1: Innovation and Simplification

"Can you share an example of when you innovated or reinvented something in a way that simplified a complex problem to its core essence? How did you challenge existing norms, and what was the impact?"

Attributes Assessed:

- Inventiveness and Creativity
- Ability to Distill Complexity into Simplicity
- Challenging Conventions

Rubric for Scoring Question 1:

- 5 (Excellent):
    - Provided a specific example of innovative thinking that simplified a complex issue.
    - Challenged existing norms significantly.
    - Resulted in substantial positive impact.

- 4 (Good):
    - Shared a clear instance of innovation and simplification.
    - Positively impacted the project or organization.
- 3 (Average):
    - Offered an example with some innovation or simplification.
    - Impact was moderate.
- 2 (Below Average):
    - Example lacked originality or effective simplification.
    - Minimal impact.
- 1 (Poor):
    - Unable to provide an example.
    - Resistant to innovation or simplification.

Question 2: Urgency, Resilience, and Relentless Pursuit

"Describe a situation where you had to take immediate action in the face of significant obstacles or setbacks. How did you handle the challenges, and what were the results?"

Attributes Assessed:

- Sense of Urgency
- Resilience and Grit
- Relentless Focus on Results

Rubric for Scoring Question 2:

- 5 (Excellent):

- ○ Detailed a high-pressure situation requiring swift action.
  - ○ Demonstrated exceptional resilience and grit.
  - ○ Overcame obstacles, leading to significant success.
- 4 (Good):
  - ○ Provided an example of acting promptly and persistently.
  - ○ Achieved positive outcomes despite challenges.
- 3 (Average):
  - ○ Example included timely action with some perseverance.
  - ○ Outcome was satisfactory.
- 2 (Below Average):
  - ○ Showed hesitation or struggled with challenges.
  - ○ Limited success.
- 1 (Poor):
  - ○ Avoided action or gave up when faced with obstacles.
  - ○ Negative results.

Question 3: Authenticity and Embracing Conflict

"Tell me about a time when you engaged in a direct, intense debate or had to be brutally honest to push an idea forward. How did you approach the situation, and what was the outcome?"

Attributes Assessed:

- Brutal Transparency and Honesty
- Willingness to Engage in Direct, Intense Debate
- Collaboration Through Conflict

Rubric for Scoring Question 3:

- 5 (Excellent):
  - Provided a specific instance of direct, honest communication in a challenging context.
  - Demonstrated the ability to handle conflict constructively.
  - Led to stronger ideas or solutions.
- 4 (Good):
  - Shared an example of honest dialogue or debate.
  - Resulted in positive outcomes.
- 3 (Average):
  - Example involved some honest communication.
  - Outcome was acceptable.
- 2 (Below Average):
  - Hesitant to be direct or engage in conflict.
  - Limited effectiveness.
- 1 (Poor):
  - Avoided honesty or mishandled conflict.
  - Negative consequences ensued.

<u>Final Steps:</u>

- Total the scores from all three questions (maximum of 15).
- Assess the results:
  - Eliminate any candidate scoring less than 3 on any question.
  - Eliminate any candidate with a total score below 10.

- Provide brief notes citing specific elements from the candidate's responses to justify your scores.

<u>Additional Interviewer Tips:</u>

- Be Mindful of Time: Keep the conversation focused within the allotted time.
- Encourage Specificity: Guide candidates to provide detailed, relevant examples.
- Active Listening: Pay attention to assess multiple attributes.
- Effective Probing: Use follow-up questions to elicit necessary details.
- Maintain Objectivity: Use the rubrics for consistent scoring.

90-Day Check-In Assessment for New Hires

Purpose

This assessment evaluates the new hire's alignment with our cultural principles, job performance, and potential at their 90-day check-in. Feedback will inform decisions about their continued employment and development within the company. Input will be collected from 3-4 colleagues who have directly worked with the new hire. Scores will be averaged, and comments summarized to provide a comprehensive evaluation.

Instructions for Colleagues

- Confidentiality: Your individual responses will be confidential and aggregated with feedback from other colleagues.
- Honesty and Objectivity: Provide honest, objective feedback based on your direct interactions with the new hire.
- Specific Examples: Include specific examples to support your ratings and comments.
- Rating Scale: For each question, rate the new hire on a scale from 1 to 5:
    - 1 = Does Not Meet Expectations
    - 2 = Below Expectations
    - 3 = Meets Expectations
    - 4 = Exceeds Expectations
    - 5 = Significantly Exceeds Expectations

Assessment Questions

Question 1: Innovation and Willingness to Challenge Conventions

"How well does the new hire demonstrate innovation, creativity, and a willingness to challenge conventions?"

Rating (1-5):

Comments: Provide examples where the new hire reimagined or reinvented a process, product, or solution in an impactful way.

Question 2: Sense of Urgency and Immediate Action

"To what extent does the new hire demonstrate a relentless sense of urgency and decisiveness in achieving results?"

Rating (1-5):

Comments: Share instances where the new hire took immediate, impactful action, cutting through obstacles to drive results.

Question 3: Authenticity, Direct Communication, and Resilience in Conflict

"How effectively does the new hire demonstrate authenticity, direct communication, and resilience, especially when engaging in challenging conversations or debates?"

Rating (1-5):

Comments: Provide examples where the new hire engaged in direct, honest dialogue or debate to push ideas forward and showed resilience in facing difficult situations.

Question 4: Clarity and Quality of Work

"How would you rate the new hire's ability to distill complex issues to their core and produce high-quality, impactful work?"

Rating (1-5):

Comments: Share examples that reflect the new hire's ability to simplify complexity, maintain clarity in their work, and deliver high standards consistently.

Question 5: Potential to Become World-Class in Their Current Role

"To what extent does the new hire demonstrate the potential to become world-class in their current position?"

Rating (1-5):

Comments: Provide observations indicating the new hire's potential for outstanding achievement and impact in their role.

Final Comments

Additional Feedback: Please share any other observations about the new hire that haven't been covered above. Focus on constructive feedback that can aid their professional development.

Strategic Principles for [A Hypothetical New Company]

Vision: We will develop energy storage technology so powerful and efficient that it will decouple human civilization from traditional power grids, enabling a sustainable future where every home, vehicle, and city can generate, store, and distribute their own clean energy, revolutionizing global energy independence.

1. Maximum Energy Efficiency: Continuously develop new technologies to achieve the highest energy efficiency possible, limited only by the laws of physics.
2. High Quality at Affordable Prices: Provide top-quality energy storage products at prices that make them accessible to a wide range of customers.
3. Scalable and Modular Solutions: Design flexible systems that can be easily scaled and adapted for use anywhere, from individual homes to entire cities.

We develop innovative, energy-efficient, and sustainable technologies to provide high-quality, user-friendly energy solutions at affordable prices. By offering scalable and modular systems that meet diverse needs—from individual homes to entire cities—we empower customers worldwide, support widespread adoption, and advance global energy independence while maintaining environmental responsibility.

26. Further reading

In my opinion, the best book on leadership is General Patton's Principles of Life & Leadership by Porter B. Williamson. If you can only read one book from this list, it should be this book. I also recommend reading Amp It Up by Frank Slootman, The Hard Thing about Hard Things and What You Do is Who You Are by Ben Horowitz, and, for an unconventional pick, What Do You Care What Other People Think? by Richard Feynman.

If you read a second book, it should be The Infinite Game by Simon Sinek. This book is, in some ways, the opposite of General Patton's. I don't agree with everything in it, particularly the emphasis on psychological safety, but it's the best description of what it means to have a vision and why it's important that I've come across. For a book that's more focused on startups (rather than legacy companies), follow it up with Zero to One by Peter Thiel.

If you read a third book, it should be Inspired by Marty Cagan. This is the OG book on product management. The second half dives a bit too deep into the details for my taste, but the description of prototype driven product discovery is a masterclass. I also recommend reading Insanely Simple by Ken Segall to learn more about designing insanely great products, and Build by Tony Faddell for a memoir style tale of a visionary product leader.

Conclusion

It is almost certainly evident from what I've written in this book that I hold a belief that has the potential to be controversial, which is that certain types of people are more likely to be successful in startups than others. And, moreover, that many of the traits that predict if someone will be successful at a startup have as much to do with their personality and values as with their background, experiences, or skills. Furthermore, these are often the opposite of the traits that would predict their success in some other environment or career. I do not deny it.

In ecology, there is a concept called a "niche". A species's niche refers to the set of conditions in an ecosystem that allows for the survival of that species. For example, the shape of a particular bird's beak may be especially well suited to gathering nectar from a particular type of flower. In ecosystems that support multiple species, each species will occupy a different niche. There is no inherent sense that one niche is better or worse than another; it just is how it is. I think this works as a useful metaphor for people as well.

There are many areas in which people can find employment. Some people choose to be scientific researchers and work in academia. Some choose to be teachers and work in elementary or high schools. Some choose to become lawyers and work at law firms, whereas other lawyers go on to work in government. Some people work in service to their country as members of the armed services. Some people choose to work as medical researchers aiming to cure whole diseases, whereas others choose to become doctors and cure individual patients. Etc. I do not believe that a person exists who has the correct combination of skills, temperament, and character to excel in every single one of these possible jobs. At least, not by the time they reach adulthood—I do generally believe that most people could develop the characteristics required for success in any particular area if they started working on them as a child. In any case, each person has to specialize. And if you are an adult then your brain has already specialized, whether you realize it or not. Although, it is somewhat unfortunate that our brains start to specialize when we are relatively young (e.g., as teenagers) before we know what we would want to do, and they are difficult to go back and change later on.

That is to say—startup life isn't for everyone. Most people do not have the risk tolerance, grit, openness, sense of urgency, ambition, and decisiveness to thrive at a startup. And that's just for working at one! An even smaller subset of people is well matched to the lifestyle of a startup founder. That's okay. Nobody is forcing you to start a company, or to work at a startup. It is a path of high risk, with a high potential for reward, but almost always fraught with pain. In this book, I've provided some recommendations that I think can help to keep this pain to a minimum should you choose to brave those dangerous waters, but I can promise that it will still be a difficult and painful journey nonetheless.

While I was working on this book, Paul Graham of Y Combinator published an essay called "Founder Mode" in which he argued that startup founders tend to run companies differently from professional managers because founders tend to stay involved in the details of their companies even as those companies grow. This essay quickly went viral, garnering both praise and condemnation. This book makes a similar argument to an even greater degree, and in much more detail, but is aimed more at the earlier stages of company building. Nevertheless, I probably don't need to say that I think startup founders should stay in the details within their area of comparative advantage for as long as they are continuing to work at their startups.

That's not to say there are no potential downsides to operating in founder mode. There are at least four obvious pitfalls that I can think of.

The first pitfall occurs when a founder attempts to stay in the details in an area in which they do not have a comparative advantage. This pitfall was covered in Chapter XXX: Manager to your advantage, so there I don't have much to add here.

The second pitfall occurs if the founder attempts to stay in the details in an area in which they do have a comparative advantage—that is, within an area in which they should stay in the details—but they have failed to hire people in that area who they work well with. If this happens, the founder will be very frustrated with their staff, and the staff will be very frustrated with the founder. Nobody will be happy. Maybe everyone will quit. This is a very big mistake; a potential startup killer. But, there are multiple ways it can happen. One way this can occur is that the founder believes one should primarily hire for skills instead of for culture and personality fit. They will find out the hard way about the error of their ways. A second way this can occur is if the founder, for one reason or another such as listening to bad advice about focusing on executive business tasks, delegates all aspects of this area of his/her company including hiring and comes to find an unfamiliar and uninviting culture when he or she returns to the details. In fact, I think this mistake is quite common, and helping founders avoid it is one of the main reasons I've written this book.

The third pitfall is that by operating in founder mode you could inadvertently teach people in your company to become helpless, to depend on you to solve all of their problems. That is, at least, the people in the areas in which you remain in the details. This is probably the best argument against operating in founder mode as your startup grows, so it's worth some consideration. There is a story that Shyam Sankar the Chief Technology Officer at Palantir invites new employees to shout "fuck off" at him at the end of orientation in order to reinforce a cultural principle highlighting a distaste for hierarchy and authority. It is important, I think, that employees at a startup take the view that anybody's problem is everybody's problem and that anybody, including and perhaps especially the founder, should contribute to solving a problem if they can. Note that I use the term "problem" broadly—like a scientist would—a problem is any unanswered question relevant to the business. Therefore, the founder should be seen in these cases as one of the rocks in the rock tumbler along with everybody else, rather than the person who owns the rock tumbler. However, I also think that the founder should consciously choose not to solve some problems even if he or she thinks they could help, as long as the problems are not too urgent or if there would be big consequences for failure. This requires the founder to show some personal discipline in identifying when to step in, and when not to step in. An executive coach may be able to help develop this capability. In addition, high agency employees are unlikely to learn helplessness because it's not in their nature. So, hiring for agency helps to mitigate this problem too.

The fourth pitfall is that operating in founder mode is difficult and you'll be working like crazy all of the time. Maybe you'll burn out. Just look at Elon Musk. He doesn't seem very happy or well adjusted. To some extent, this can be mitigated by only going into the details within your areas of comparative advantage. It's likely that these are areas you enjoy, and if you aren't happy working super hard on problems you enjoy and are good at then I'm afraid to say you're probably not going to make it as a startup founder anyway. In addition, working hard alongside people you get along with is often great fun, so there's another reason to focus on hiring people you like working with. Moreover, if you've done the job I told you to in Chapter 1 by crafting a big important vision that you're intensely passionate about, you'll be able to weather the long hours without too much difficulty. Aside from that, all I have to offer are two pieces of advice. First, try to get a full night's sleep every night. Sleep is very important for the proper functioning of your brain, and the proper functioning of your brain is important for your startup. So don't try to emulate Elon and sleep on the factory floor. Second, find an activity you can do each day that lets you shut your brain off for 30 minutes or so. You could try meditation, yoga, weightlifting, running, boxing —whatever activity you enjoy doing that forces you to stop thinking about other things and only focus on doing that activity. Sometimes, stress can turn into recurring thought patterns that get worse and worse as they rattle around in your brain, but the right activity can short circuit your neural pathways and get your head back in the game.

Founder mode and manager mode are not the only modes you can find yourself in, although they are the most common. A third mode I discovered at some point is succession mode.

Succession mode is what happens when you make the difficult, conscious decision to change from founder mode into manager mode in order to make room for somebody else to step up and take the lead. You'll know when it's time, and you'll probably feel a bit guilty about it, but you have to do what's best for both you and your company. Succession mode is like being a parent, taking off your child's floaties, pushing them into the deep end, and then watching closely to see if they are able to swim on their own. It's stressful for both you and the child, but if you've done the right things leading up to it they will swim just fine and be better for it.

When the day came that I officially stepped down as CEO, it felt (I imagine) like sending a child off to college. A time of strong, mixed emotions. Happy because they've graduated to the next stage in their life. Worried that you didn't do enough to prepare them. Proud that they're going out into the world on their own. Sad because the days when you spent all your time together are in the past. Excited to hear about their new adventures and accomplishments. A bit lost because you don't know what to do next. But, life is measured by the number of one way doors you walk through. It's in those moments that the clock ticks forward. Because the old saying that when one door closes another opens is wrong; when one door closes, two must open. The entropy of the universe must increase.